a twist i

pigh s

tale

a twist in the pighunter's tale

Charger Morrison

REED

Published by Reed Books, a division of Reed Publishing (NZ) Ltd, 39 Rawene Rd, Birkenhead, Auckland. Associated companies, branches and representatives throughout the world.

ISBN 0 7900 0629 4

Cover and text designed by Michele Stutton
Illustrations by Kerry Robertson

First published 1998

Printed in New Zealand

For LDR for reasons that go on for ever.

Preface

Best read this before you start.

Apart from changing names, dates and locations everything you read from here on is true apart from the bits I made up which bear no resemblance to the truth whatsoever. But a word of warning: the bits you're likely to dismiss as being outright lies could well be the true bits. In fact, chances are, they are, and that's the truth.

Contents

CHAPTER 1

Delayed Reaction

Jimmy O'Connor was born before the turn of the twentieth century just outside Palmerston North and died in 1956 just outside Wanganui. But he'd crammed a lot of living into his seventy-odd years. You could say Jimmy was of the stuff of which legends are made; and you'd be right too. But Jimmy didn't become a legendary figure. Legends are often made through good press agents and influential friends in high places, and Jimmy didn't have either of these. What he did have was an unquenchable sense of adventure and the backbone to go find it.

Before his sixteenth birthday, Jimmy crossed the Tasman and took a job on a cattle station in northern New South Wales. He wasn't much of a horseman at first, but after taking a few falls and a fair amount of good-natured ribbing from his mates, Jimmy learnt to hold his own alongside his Aussie stockmen — crack riders to a man.

At the outbreak of the First World War Jimmy lied about his age and signed on with the renowned Australian Light Horse Regiment. He saw action in the Middle East and Europe and was awarded the Military Medal for Conspicuous Gallantry. He was also twice mentioned in despatches and got promoted to sergeant. If Jimmy had stayed on in the army, maybe things would have panned out differently. But he didn't. At war's end he returned to his old job back on the cattle station, his only regret being that many of his former mates hadn't returned with him. They lay in unmarked graves in the battlefields of Gallipoli and the Somme and Jimmy would often shed a tear in remembering them.

After a year or so he was given the job of station manager. In addition to a substantial rise in salary there was a three-bedroom house thrown in and the boss promised to go halves with him on any unbranded cattle they brought in on the annual muster. Over the next ten years Jimmy worked hard and prospered. He built up a sizeable herd and bank account and if he'd been the kind of bloke to socialise, there's little doubt he would have been regarded as the most eligible bachelor in the state. But socialising wasn't Jimmy's thing.

When he wasn't working he was hunting. Kangaroos, foxes, dingos and wild pigs, mostly. Usually on horseback and armed with a Lee Enfield .303, Jimmy took a fearful toll of the wildlife that abounded in that part of the country. Hunting was a form of recreation for him, but it was also a necessity. Droughts were common, and the 'roos and pigs competed with the cattle for grass. It was a lonely life, but Jimmy didn't mind that. He never tired of his own company, and felt at ease in his surroundings.

Despite this, Jimmy's boss didn't want his favourite station manager going bush happy on him, so he bought Jimmy a return train ticket to Sydney and insisted he take a well-deserved holiday. 'A few weeks in the big smoke will make a new man of you, Jimmy,' his boss told him.

Jimmy didn't think he needed to be made into a new man but he went anyway, and that's how he came to meet up with Joyce. Joyce was a city girl, brash and brassy, who liked a good time and didn't seem to mind how she got it — or what anyone else had to do to provide it for her. She was also one hell of a looker, and Jimmy was smitten. There was a whirlwind courtship followed by a registry office wedding and a week-long honeymoon in the Blue Mountains before Jimmy took his bride home to his three-bedroom house in the outback.

Joyce was not impressed. In fact she hated the place right from the start. As far as she was concerned, the heat, dust and flies had been put there just to make her life miserable, and she complained continuously about the isolation and boredom. The nearest town was Clayburn, some 40 miles away, and in an effort to make life more bearable Jimmy made the trip every week so that Joyce could do some shopping and as often as not they'd go to the picture theatre, or visit friends. But it was never enough for Joyce, who was missing the high life and bright lights of the city. And she let everybody know it.

To add to Jimmy's troubles there was a depression on. Money was tight, stock prices were at an all-time low, and northern New South Wales was facing its third consecutive year of drought. Jimmy and Joyce had never known much in the way of marital bliss but when his bride of just two years did a runner on him, Jimmy was pretty well crushed by it all. Joyce had taken off with Bill Phillips, who was a representative for some paint and wallpaper company in Sydney, and the two of them were living together in Clayburn.

Those who knew Jimmy half expected him to drive into Clayburn and make a hospital case out of Bill Phillips. But no such thing. Once he'd got over the initial shock, Jimmy didn't seem to harbour any bitterness, and was quite philosophical about it, if anything. Reckoned it was really all for the best as Joyce had never been happy with station life and he would never have been able to live in town.

The scandal was the main topic of discussion among the locals for the next few weeks, but after that people lost interest and got on with their lives, as Jimmy readjusted to being a bachelor again. Something which he had no trouble doing.

In fact it was the general consensus of opinion around the district that Jimmy was looking happier and healthier than ever, and seemed to be doing better for himself all round. The drought had broken, there'd been an upturn in the beef market and Jimmy had found a market for his kangaroo skins.

It wasn't enough to get rich on but you could call it a fairly lucrative sideline all the same. As for Bill Phillips and Joyce, they were still getting along okay but Joyce wasn't living the high life she'd expected. She hadn't been able to get a job in Clayburn as hoped, and although Bill was making enough for them to live on there wasn't too much left over for the luxuries. There was some talk that this was putting a strain on their relationship.

Whether or not Bill and Joyce would have lived happily ever after, or gone their separate ways, will always be open to conjecture as they were both killed in an horrific accident. It seemed that Bill kept large quantities of paint and thinners in a shed in his back garden, which he also used as an office. It was pretty volatile stuff, especially the thinners, but as neither he nor Joyce smoked, the practice was never considered dangerous.

Then one day, for no apparent reason, while the two of them were in the office, there was an almighty explosion which killed them both instantly. There was an investigation and an inquest which gave a verdict of death by misadventure.

The police called around to see Jimmy. There was no actual evidence of foul play, but in view of everything that had happened, they certainly had their suspicions. Jimmy wasn't too happy about them questioning him.

'You jokers have got nothing on me,' he told them. 'I was at the saleyards at the time of the explosion, bidding for a prize stud bull. Ask around, you'll see.'

The police did just that, and according to any number of witnesses Jimmy was at the saleyards at the time of the explosion, and as he had stated, he was putting in the winning bid for a stud Aberdeen Angus bull.

About a month after the funeral Jimmy surprised everybody by leaving the district. He packed a few things into his old Ford and headed north, to take up buffalo and crocodile shooting. It must have been hard on a bloke taking this on with no experience, but Jimmy never lacked for guts and determination, and by all accounts he did all right for himself.

There was even a rumour that whilst prospecting one day for lack of something to do, he'd struck gold. This rumour was strengthened by Jimmy sending enough money home to his parents who were still living in Palmerston North for them to pay off their mortgage, and then coming home himself.

Shortly after, he bought a property in the Wanganui River valley. I was only about five years old at the time, but I was able to piece together most of Jimmy's history whilst growing up by eavesdropping on conversations between my old man and our next door neighbour, Ted Thompson. Ted was also from Palmerston North originally, and he'd known Jimmy's parents for years. They still kept in touch.

Hearing all these stories about Jimmy made him sound like a cross between Rambo and the Man from Snowy River, so when I got to actually meet him at about age twelve, I was just a little disappointed. Jimmy was so ordinary looking. Not a bit like I imagined. He stood about five foot nine, neither fat nor thin, with sandy-coloured hair and a broken nose which he said he'd got when working as a sparring partner for Les Darcy, a famous Australian middleweight contender for the world title. I can't remember whether I believed him or not, but it didn't matter much because I wasn't to meet up with Jimmy again until about ten years later.

Jimmy had carried on in much the same way as ever, working his farm and for the most part keeping himself to himself. He became something of a recluse. Not what you would call unfriendly, but at the same time never going out of his way to mix in. He never attended any of our socials at Christmas or New Year, and if he ever received an invitation to a twenty-first birthday or somebody's wedding anniversary, he always courteously declined.

So when Jimmy showed up at one of the early pighunting competitions we'd organised with a scoffing great brute of a boar strapped over the bonnet of his truck, it just about floored us all. None of us had any idea that Jimmy was a pighunter, but the proof was right there. A fair dinkum Captain Cooker complete with a murderous set of hooks, shot neatly between the ears and weighing in at 351 pounds. If it wasn't for the fact that Jimmy hadn't paid his entry fee of ten bob, he would have walked away with the first prize consisting of twenty five quid and a dozen bottles of beer.

When told of this, Jimmy just shrugged good-naturedly and said he'd remember next time. And that's exactly what he did when we had another competition six weeks later. On that occasion Jimmy showed up with two boars, his biggest weighing in at 298 pounds. It was pipped at the post by Sammy Mita's grunter, which pulled the needle down to 301 pounds. Jimmy had to be content with second prize of five quid. But his other boar, which wasn't even in the running for size, took first place for best set of tusks, which gave Jimmy another cash prize of five quid and a half dozen bottles of beer.

In typical fashion Jimmy wasn't keen on sticking around for the social we had planned, but the boys were full of questions. How and where was he getting his pigs? What kind of dog was he using? How big was his pack? Did he want to sell any of them? and so on. But Jimmy wasn't giving anything away. He went all coy and evasive. 'You can't expect a bloke to give away all his secrets,' he joked, 'especially when he gets to my age.'

I had to admit to being just a little curious over Jimmy's success, but what really had me mystified was the manner in which all three boars brought in by Jimmy had been killed. That is, despatched by way of a single bullet through the top of the head and as near as dammit to dead centre between the ears.

This was something to wonder at in itself, even allowing for Jimmy's renowned marksmanship. But there was more. I'd also noticed that the exit wounds on all three were directly below those of entry, which meant that Jimmy would have to be directly above the boars when firing, and holding the rifle dead vertical.

Now it's fair to say that, under certain conditions, such a situation could occur. Like having his dogs bail a pig at the bottom of a narrow gut or something similar, but it wouldn't happen that often, and the chances of it happening three times in a row would have to be remote if not downright impossible.

We had another competition scheduled for Labour Weekend and even though it was more than two months away it came as no surprise when I noticed Jimmy putting his name down for it and handing over the entrance fee to Barry Simms, the club treasurer. I decided against saying anything to anyone, partly because I didn't really have anything to say, but mostly because I wanted to wait for the day and have a look at any boars that Jimmy brought in.

In the meantime I would try and nut things out for myself. For starters, if Jimmy was hunting the bush at the back of his property then it would be quite an achievement for a man of his years as that bit of country was about as rugged as it could get. Then there was the question of his dogs. Where were they? Mick Lawson, Jimmy's neighbour, reckoned he hadn't seen any extra dogs on Jimmy's place; just the same old pair, Boss and Skipper, neither of which would ever make a pig dog. They had enough trouble finding their way out of the stockyards.

Perhaps the most puzzling thing of all was what had prompted Jimmy's sudden desire to enter pighunting competitions at his time of life — and it was sudden. Not for all the years he had lived in the valley had Jimmy ever shown any interest in the sport, preferring instead to channel his energies into fly fishing, which he was good at, and target shooting, which he was very good at.

Was the prize money a determining factor? Twenty-five quid ($50) doesn't sound like much these days, but back in the early 1950s it was close on to two months' wages for a farmhand. I didn't want to go snooping around Jimmy's property, but just three days before the start of our Labour Weekend competition Jimmy put himself out of action by tripping over a loose step on his verandah and wrenching his ankle. Fortunately nothing was broken, but he was going to be out of action for at least a week, so going round to give him back his entrance fee and offer a word of sympathy gave me a good excuse for being there.

I called round next day late in the afternoon half expecting to find Jimmy laid up or something, but there he was, hobbling back from the woodshed to his kitchen with an armful of manuka. He smiled a greeting as I pulled up in the old Chevy. 'G'day, Charger, what brings you out to this neck of the woods?'

'Thought I'd call round to see how the invalid was getting along,' I answered, turning off the ignition and yanking on the handbrake.

Jimmy smiled again, looking just a little embarrassed. 'I didn't think I was important enough to get a visit from the club president. You'd better come in and have a brew. I've got the billy boiling.'

I followed Jimmy into his kitchen, noticing how neat and clean and tidy it was compared to mine. I rolled a couple of smokes while Jimmy poured out two mugs of strong black tea and stirred in liberal quantities of condensed milk and sugar — enough to produce instant cavities.

'The boys and I thought it only fair to refund your entry fee, Jimmy,' I said, taking a sip of tea. 'What with you being out of action, thought it might cheer you up a bit.'

The look on Jimmy's face said he was anything but cheered. 'You mean you mongrels are putting a man out of the running without giving him a chance? Pretty dirty trick if you ask me.'

I was just a bit hacked off with Jimmy's attitude; quite taken aback by it in fact.

'Just taihoa there a minute, mate,' I told him. 'The boys thought they were doing you a favour by refunding your money. It's not as if we had to, we just thought it was fair. What with you being out of action and everything. And now the only thanks we get is having you accuse us of pulling dirty tricks.'

Jimmy gave a half-hearted shrug. I could see he was working up to an apology. 'Fair enough, Charger,' he sighed. 'I was out of line with what I said; and I'm sorry. But I still want to have a go in the competition. I reckon I have every right.'

'Sure you do, Jimmy,' I agreed, 'but how are you going to compete with your ankle all swollen up like that?'

Jimmy gave another shrug. 'The competition is still three days away. A man can do a lot of healing in three days.'

Not for the life of me could I see how Jimmy was going to be in a fit enough state to take on the hills, but as he'd said, he had every right to try. 'Okay, Jimmy,' I smiled. 'I think you're a stubborn old coot that hasn't got a chance in hell, but the best of luck anyway.'

As there was nothing more to say on the subject, nothing more was said, though Jimmy's hostile outburst when he thought he'd been denied entry into the competition was still nagging at me a bit. I spent the next hour carting firewood from Jimmy's woodshed and stacking it by his back door while he boiled the billy again.

I couldn't stay too long after that because of work commitments. 'But ring me if you need anything,' I offered, walking out the door, 'and keep off that ankle as much as possible.'

'Yeah, I'll do that, Charger,' he said, hobbling along behind me and nearly tripping over the loose board in the verandah for the second time in as many days.

'I'll bring my tools next time and fix that step for you, Jimmy,' I promised. I was about to turn the ignition on the old Chevy when the sound of a single shot rang out. 'That was close, Jimmy,' I said. 'Sounded like it came from just behind your boundary fence. I'd better go up and have a look.'

Jimmy hastily dismissed the idea. 'There's no need for that, Charger. It's just some deerstalker out for a bit of meat for the pot.'

'You don't know that for sure, Jimmy,' I argued. 'It could be some young hoon with more bullets than brains, blasting off just for the hell of it. Whoever he is he's a bit too close to the farmland for my liking. We've all had our share of stock losses through this sort of thing.'

Jimmy was starting to look uncomfortable. 'There's still no need for you to go up there, though,' he insisted. 'Whoever it was is most probably gone now anyway.'

It was obvious that for some reason or other Jimmy didn't want me to investigate, which made me all the more determined to do so. 'Think I'll go and have a look anyway, mate,' I said, and moved off before he could make any more objections.

I was about halfway to the fenceline when I noticed Jimmy was hobbling along behind me. Silly old fool was going to do himself an injury, nothing surer. I didn't have a clue what I was looking for, but somehow I knew that the shot I'd heard had nothing to do with any wandering deerstalker, and the boar lying under the fence with the old .303 Lee Enfield tied above it had everything to do with it.

The pigs had found an opening in Jimmy's fenceline and no doubt had been helping themselves to a feed of turnips and chou moellier, so Jimmy had rigged up a trip wire connected to the trigger of the .303 so it would fire on contact. It was a real neat set-up, quite ingenious in fact, but Jimmy had been breaking the rules of the contest we'd been holding which clearly stated that all pigs entered had to be taken by way of 'fair chase', which Jimmy's set-up clearly didn't comply with.

I waited until he came limping his way up alongside of me whereupon he sat down on the grass staring in silence at his pasturelands below. More than five minutes passed before he said anything, offering nothing in the way of excuses. 'It's just an improvement on an idea I picked up in Belgium during the Great War,' he explained. 'We'd take a town or village in the morning, then the Germans would put in a counterattack in the afternoon and we'd be on the retreat out of there. So some of the boys would leave rifles rigged up to fire when someone opened a door or hit a trip wire when walking into a room. I don't suppose it worked often enough to make any difference, but it gave the Hun something to worry about. Sometimes if we were in too much of a hurry to empty out our ammo dumps, we'd set up our cigarette bombs. And they always provided fireworks.'

Just for a moment, Jimmy smiled at the memory before returning to the subject in hand. 'I suppose this little lot is going to get me blacklisted; what with getting caught by the club president, of all people.'

'Why did you do it, Jimmy?' I asked. 'Was it the money?'

Jimmy shook his head. 'No, mate. I've got enough put by to see me out. I suppose it was just the thrill of putting one over all you young jokers and being the centre of attention. It just got the better of me.'

As club president I had to make a decision, and after all these years I believe I did the right thing, by both the club and Jimmy himself. 'Tell you what, Jimmy,' I said. 'Nobody ever need know about this. It can be our secret. But you make an anonymous donation to the club for the same amount you took us for, and if you enter any more contests, you stick to the rules. Fair enough?'

Jimmy sounded relieved. 'Fair enough, Charger.'

I gutted the boar and slowly we made our way down to the homestead where I hung it in Jimmy's meat safe. He wouldn't have to worry about dog tucker for a while. A little after that, Jimmy brought out two mugs of steaming tea. We sat on the back porch watching the sunset, and I remembered something Jimmy had mentioned up by the fenceline. 'By the way, Jimmy,' I asked, 'what's a cigarette bomb?'

'I'll show you,' he said.

With that he hobbled inside and came out a few minutes later with a packet of Capstan cigarettes, a box of matches and an empty one-gallon kerosene tin. 'Right, pay attention,' he said. 'This is what we used to leave behind in our ammo dumps to blow them up before the Jerries could get their hands on them. Simple, but effective,' he added, with some degree of pride.

I watched as Jimmy lit the cigarette then, opening the box of matches, placed the unlit end against the heads of the matches before closing the box just enough to hold the cigarette securely. He removed the screw top from the kerosene tin, then placed the box of matches over the opening. 'Now tell me, Charger,' he asked, 'what's going to happen when the cigarette burns down to the matches?'

'All the matches will burst into flames,' I answered.

Jimmy slapped me on the shoulder. 'That's right! Now imagine that tin is full of petrol — or paint thinners, or something else flammable. What would happen then?'

I could see it all — the matches bursting into flames, igniting the fumes which in turn would ignite the petrol in the can — one almighty explosion. 'And the cigarette,' I said, 'takes a few minutes to burn down, so a man has plenty of time to get well clear of it.'

Jimmy smiled a smile that I'll never forget. 'That's right, Charger,' he said, 'a man could be miles away, playing golf or taking a Sunday stroll — or even down at the stock sale putting in a bid for an Aberdeen Angus stud bull.'

OTEL

CHAPTER 2

Settling Accounts

It was a sad day for everybody in the valley when we buried old Bob Eamon, especially for us younger blokes. As far as we were concerned old Bob had been the best thing since school holidays had been invented. While we were teenagers growing up through those restless, uncertain years of the Second World War, Bob formed and coached our football and cricket teams, acted as Scout Master, and when my old man had the tractor accident which put him out of action for almost a year, Bob stepped in as our boxing instructor. None of us knew it at the time but Bob had been quite a scrapper in his youth. Rumour had it that while on a brief visit over in Australia in 1908 he'd been given the job of sparring partner to the great Jack Johnson before he'd fought Tommy Burns for the World Heavyweight title. Bob himself would neither deny nor confirm the story but if you'd seen the classic footwork and precision-timed punching he demonstrated when putting us through our paces you would have thought it more than possible.

In fact, if it hadn't been for Bob I doubt I would have made it into the North Island finals that year. I was due to fight Billy Keene and Billy had one of the best right crosses in the country, which meant bad news for me because the only way I could stop a right cross in those days was by putting my chin in the way. I discussed it with Bob and he showed me a countermove so beautifully simple, even I could do it.

Night after night Bob threw right crosses at me until I was seeing them in my sleep. Each time he threw one I had to step in hard with my right foot, turn sideways and deliver a right uppercut. The old bloke must have taken me through that procedure a thousand times, but it paid off on the night. Billy had been skiting how he was going to knock me out in two rounds and he might have done too, except I spoilt his plans a bit by knocking him out in round one.

The way Bob congratulated me you would have thought I'd won a world title all on my own, but that's the kind of bloke he was, never wanting to take credit, and I've got to admit it felt pretty good being in the limelight and seeing my name in the *Herald*.

After the war ended there was a surplus of .303 rifles and ammunition going cheap and before long most of us young jokers were taking to the bush every weekend hunting deer for the skin market and for the one shilling per snout government bounty that was being paid at the time. There were a lot of animals about in those early post-war years so picking up enough skins or snouts to make a decent-sized cheque wasn't too difficult, but we knew it wouldn't last, and it didn't.

Access to the valley became easier and hordes of hunters from the cities and towns were coming in literally by the carload. The place was getting thrashed. The deer and pigs were being thinned out and those left were becoming very wary and harder to hunt. It got so bad that we were having trouble picking up the odd deer or pig for dog tucker. Although we wouldn't admit it the trouble was none of us had learned to be hunters, not in the true sense that is, simply because we never had to be. In the early years all a man had to do was take a stroll along the river to find game around almost every bend, but by the time the 1950s rolled around that had become a thing of the past. Only the clued-up hunters were scoring and we didn't have any clues, but good old Bob came to the rescue.

He took us into the bush and showed us things that we never even knew existed. 'Deer and pigs are a lot like us,' he said. 'They like to keep warm and dry and not too far away from food and water, so if you think along these lines you can narrow down your hunting area instead of wandering around aimlessly. Unlike us,' he went on, 'wild animals depend on their acute senses of smell and hearing rather than their eyesight to warn them of approaching danger, so keep the sun at your back, the wind in your face and move quietly.'

Under Bob's guidance we were soon getting the hang of things, sussing out all the hot spots and learning to use the wind, but we were all having trouble with that 'move quietly' thing. Bob would glide through the bush without so much as rustling a leaf while we followed behind making more noise than a regiment of Grenadier Guards marching over broken glass in hobnailed boots. But Bob never lost patience with any of us provided he could see we were trying. 'Keep working on it, it'll come,' he promised, and it did.

It wasn't a gradual process either, not like you'd think it would be. You'd spend weeks sneaking and creeping through the bush with no apparent signs of improvement then one day everything would fall into place. Without even realising it you'd be weaving through the fern and supplejack effortlessly and as silent as the rising mist; a real neat feeling.

Bob knew a few things about pig dogs too and could pick a potential champion out of a litter with unfailing accuracy every time. According to Bob the first thing a pup had to have was plenty of black inside its mouth. Usually half the litter would meet this qualification so then he'd move on to the next stage by picking each one up by the scruff of the neck and giving it a shake. Any that squealed were put aside. By this time he'd often have just two pups left to choose from so he'd put them both in a cardboard box then sit back and roll himself a smoke. Being in a strange environment the pups would kick up a fuss but one of them would always settle down first and go to sleep and that was the one Bob would pick because he reckoned it showed a stable temperament which he regarded as one of the most important attributes of a pig dog.

How much stock you want to put in Bob's method of picking out a potential champion is over to you but I've been using it for almost fifty years now and it hasn't put me crook yet. Although he had a good pack himself and did a lot of pighunting with them, there were times when Bob would leave his dogs at home. Like at the first sign of rain in summer after a long dry spell. Bob would head off for the open grassy tops and always come back with plenty of pork. If we'd used the brains we were born with we could have worked it out for ourselves but we didn't, so Bob had to explain it all.

'There's nothing like summer rain to bring pigs out into the open,' he'd tell us. 'It gives them a chance to cool off and rid themselves of lice. The rain also softens the ground and brings the worms closer to the surface which makes it easier for them to root around for a feed. Under these circumstances, you're better off without dogs. Just sneak along the bush edge with a rifle or wait in ambush. If you're any good you'll drop two or three before they get under cover.'

We all had a go at trying Bob's method after that and even if it wasn't as much fun as running the dogs it invariably proved profitable when conditions were right. Another trick Bob showed us was how to hunt at night without a spotlight. All you needed was a scope-sighted rifle and a full moon and you could pick the pigs off no trouble because the scope would drag all the light in. It was almost like shooting in the daytime. This method was especially effective in areas where pigs had become 'light shy'. There were a whole lot of other things Bob showed us, and out of gratitude and respect for the man I've tried to pass them on over the years to other young hunters.

After the funeral our neighbour Ted Thompson took it on himself to sort out Bob's estate and affairs, notifying next of kin and that sort of thing. As far as any of us knew Bob didn't have any relatives so it was a real eye-opener when we found out he had a son living in Christchurch who owned a guest house of all things. According to the records Bob had married a Miss Eileen Swartz in 1919 and in 1920 the union had been blessed with the birth of their son, James.

This had us really curious because we all thought we knew everything there was to know about Bob, but there was more to come. Ted was pretty good at finding things out and knew enough of the right people in all the right places to help him. Digging deeper into the old records we found that Bob's wife had divorced him in 1926 for desertion and had remarried somebody called Simon Bowden. Also, Bob's son James, after turning 21, had legally changed his name from Eamon to Bowden. It was all quite involved.

None of us could see Bob as the type to desert a wife and child and we felt sure that there had to be more to the story than what the records showed. Ted was of the opinion that Bob and his wife had separated by mutual agreement and after the required period of time stipulated by law, his wife had filed for divorce on the grounds of desertion even though Bob hadn't deserted her in the way the records indicated. 'You have to remember the divorce laws were a lot stricter back then,' Ted explained, 'and married couples had to resort to all kinds of things to get a divorce. My guess is that Bob and his wife arranged the whole thing between them. It was a common enough practice in those days,' Ted concluded confidently, and we were all happy to believe it.

Bob's son was contacted and three weeks after the funeral he showed up to have a look at the property that his father had farmed for the last twenty years and had left him in his will. James Bowden was nothing like his father and he rubbed most of us up the wrong way right from the start. It was obvious that as a big city man he regarded us as a bunch of ignorant country hicks and reckoned the best thing he could do with his father's property was put a match to it.

This didn't exactly endear Mr Bowden to the rest of us because we all knew how hard Bob had worked on the place. Admittedly it wasn't much of a farm but that wasn't Bob's fault. In those days a lot of properties failed to realise their full potential because of a cobalt deficiency in the soil which we were only just starting to learn about. Bob's neighbour, Frank Avery, had the same problem and for the three years he'd been on the property, which he'd inherited from some relative or other, he'd worked from dawn to dusk, seven days a week, just to scrape a living.

At first it seemed as though James Bowden was going to put the place on the market but after talking to some property developers from town he announced he was going to turn it into a hunting lodge for tourist hunters. This idea came as something of a surprise to us simple valley folk, but once we thought it out it didn't seem such a bad idea at that. Although Bob's property had been about 3000 acres all up, only a third of it had ever been cleared. The rest was rugged bush, about as rugged as you could get, and it was well known that Bob had had more deer and wild pigs running on his place than sheep. In addition to this the property backed onto, and gave easy access to, thousands of acres of Crown land where game numbers were still quite high.

James Bowden didn't waste any time putting his plans into effect, which I suppose was commendable, but he upset quite a few people doing it, which wasn't so commendable. It wasn't very wise either. Without even bothering to introduce himself properly he told Frank Avery to get his fences put in order because he didn't want any of Frank's stock straying onto his property. He also told Frank that he couldn't take any more short cuts through the place when shifting his sheep down to the road paddock like he'd been doing for years. This meant that Frank had to fork out a lot of time and expense putting in a new track down to the road and he wasn't too pleased about that.

The next people to be upset with James Bowden were every pighunter, duckshooter and deerstalker in the district. Inside of a month he had a dozen or so 'No Trespassing' and 'No Shooting' signs plastered all over the property and absolutely no one was allowed to set foot on the place. We could understand him not wanting a lot of indiscriminate shooting on his own property but he even went so far as to deny us access through to the Crown land, which we thought was a bit on the nose. The only other access we had was on the western side of the valley and that meant a half day's hike.

We tried reasoning with him but it was just a waste of time. He wouldn't even let Max Griffin go through to search for a dog he had lost even though Max wasn't carrying a firearm and told Bowden he had no intention of hunting. Max never saw his dog again and a rumour got round that Bowden had shot it and dumped the remains in his offal pit but we had no way of knowing anything for sure. The only thing we could do about Bowden was ignore him and this caused him more problems than anything we could have thought up. To get the property tidied up and resembling anything like a hunting lodge James Bowden needed a big labour force but none of us was going to work for him at any price.

He got so desperate he had to hire a crew of painters and carpenters from Auckland in the finish and the only fencers he could get were a couple of no-hopers from around Turangi way who charged him twice the going rate for a third grade job.

Before too long quite a few of the young blokes in the Auckland crew he'd hired started getting homesick for the bright city lights and walked off the job. On top of this most of the work that was done wasn't up to standard and the building inspector demanded it be done again. Despite this and other hassles Bowden still managed to make progress. In just over three months he'd demolished the old homestead along with the woolshed and implement shed and replaced them with a flash new four-bedroomed house and half a dozen fully self-contained cabins. He also had some stables built for the riding horses he'd bought so his prospective clients wouldn't have to walk anywhere.

The whole enterprise had to be costing Bowden a mint and he must have borrowed to the hilt but he didn't seem too worried about it. In fact he was quite confident he'd recoup his outlay in the first year and going by the prices he intended charging his overseas clients, you could believe it. As soon as his flash new house was finished, Bowden sent for his missus, and we didn't go much on her either. When Ted's wife sent over a batch of scones and some fruit chutney as a gesture of welcome, Bowden's wife sent it back with a curt note about 'being particular' of what she ate. She wasn't interested in joining the women's bowling team either, or taking part in any of their fund-raising projects for the new playcentre we were trying to get started. Like her husband, she made it quite clear that she considered us below her social status and apart from when she made the occasional visit to the store, we hardly saw anything of her.

The next person to show up at the Bowdens' was an elderly looking bloke who we thought was Bowden's father-in-law, but we weren't even close. The old bloke, Clive Mundy by name, had been employed by the Bowdens for some years as a handyman/gardener at their guest house in Christchurch, and was more or less going to be similarly employed at the hunting lodge. It was a while before we got to meet Clive because the Bowdens had him working all hours of daylight and half the night too.

When we did finally meet Clive he seemed a real good sort, nothing like the Bowdens. If anything, he reminded us of old Bob quite a bit because of the way he liked spending what little spare time he had with us young blokes. Like Bob, Clive knew his way around in the bush and showed us some pretty amazing stuff. His fish traps were really something — as near as dammit to infallible and totally undetectable which they had to be because they were also highly illegal. He took us down to the river one day to demonstrate.

The first thing he did was cut himself a pile of manuka stakes between three and four feet long, about two inches thick and sharpened to a point at one end. This task over, he then scanned the river for what he called a 'shute'. We would have helped him find one except none of us knew what it was or what we were supposed to do when we found one. 'You blokes just watch for the time being,' Clive told us, which was a waste of time because that's all we'd been doing anyway. But we did learn something. We found out that a 'shute' was a narrow strip of water in the main part of the current which is deeper and runs slower. They're easy enough to spot once you know what to look for. 'The trout always know where they are,' Clive explained, 'and they always use them when swimming upstream because they don't have to work so hard against the flow.'

Once we'd digested that lot, Clive waded out to the shute he'd chosen and started hammering the stakes into the riverbed, side by side, about an inch apart. His trap consisted of two sides of these manuka stakes, something like a picket fence, starting off three feet wide at the entrance and narrowing into a bottleneck shape just three inches wide at the narrow end which was facing upstream and blocked off. The whole thing was about six feet long and took a lot of time to set up. But as Clive pointed out the time factor didn't really matter because once you had the trap set you could leave it there for months. The only two things to remember were to make sure you hammered the stakes down below the water line so no sharp-eyed ranger spotted it and to keep the trap open when you weren't using it. This was of major importance because those traps worked really well, as we found out, and there was no point in trapping a load of fish unless you had use for them.

Using the same principle, but on a bigger and stronger scale, Clive showed us how to trap deer and pigs with them too. The trick was not just to put them on the track that you knew was being used by deer and pigs, but to put them at the bottom of a steep run. The animals would usually be picking up a bit of steam at these points and would be well inside the trap before they knew it. Clive's traps worked so well that in later years when live capture of deer became profitable a few of the mates I'd grown up with used them and had better results than the blokes with the commercially made ones.

Clive was a dab hand at snares too. He used copper wire and caught possums, rabbits and even wood pigeons with them. I used to wonder where Clive had picked up all his ideas from; he seemed to know so much about the bush and the habits of animals. My old man reckoned it would have been during the years of the Great Depression, which really didn't tell me much, but that was typical of my old man, who either blamed or attributed everything either on, or to, the Great Depression. Anyone could tell it was the most meaningful experience of his life. He never shut up about it. I'd even go so far as to say he was genuinely sorry when it ended. It didn't really matter where Clive had got so clued up on snares and traps and the bush and things like that, the thing that had us all wondering was why he stayed with the Bowdens. He was a top-notch carpenter, painter, mechanic and gardener, and was a passable farrier too, but the Bowdens didn't appear to appreciate him even a little bit. They always talked down to him and certainly didn't overpay him. He never worked less than a twelve-hour day and was lucky to get one day off a month.

Bruce Wellam who did the mail run reckoned that Clive was more or less obliged to stay with the Bowdens because he'd have a hard time getting another job owing to his age but that couldn't have been the reason. Several of the big property owners in the valley had asked Clive to come and work for them and Ted Thompson had even offered him the manager's job on his place with good wages, his own cottage and all the usual perks thrown in but Clive had politely refused them all. It was hard to imagine but perhaps Clive was happy with his lot.

Occasionally the Bowdens would take off for a week to check things out with their guest house in Christchurch and I'd call in to see Clive, give him a hand with whatever it was he was doing and then talk him into coming out on a pig hunt. About a month before the Bowdens were due for the grand opening of their hunting lodge they took off for Christchurch and left Clive to shift two truckloads of furniture into the main house and cabins all on his lonesome, so Ted, Sammy Mita and I called in to lend a hand.

Apart from a couple of chests which I assumed contained personal effects, the Bowdens had labelled each piece of furniture to say where it was supposed to go. This made the job easier and we had everything in place by lunchtime except for the two chests. They were too heavy for one man, so while Ted and Clive took an end each of one, Sammy and I struggled with the other one. I'm sure it was the heaviest as we were really heaving to get it up the verandah steps. We just about had it to the top when the handle on Sammy's end came off. I couldn't hang on to it and it went tumbling down the steps. The lid burst open and a whole lot of papers and stuff were strewn everywhere and blown around in the wind. But Clive saw the funny side of it.

It was only stuff belonging to the Bowdens and we were laughing and joking while running around collecting it when I happened to look over at Clive. He'd picked up some official-looking papers and wasn't laughing anymore; in fact he was looking quite grim about things. Sammy and Ted noticed it too and when Clive said he'd give the pighunting a miss that day we didn't try to talk him out of it. We stayed just long enough for a quick beer and tried to lighten the atmosphere but it was a lost cause. Clive just wasn't in the mood for anything except being alone so we left, promising to drop him off a nice piece of wild pork on our way back.

Neither Ted, Sammy nor I discussed it, but we were all wondering what it was that had upset Clive so much. I called round to see him two days later and he seemed happier but said he was too busy to go hunting and asked me if I had any maps of the area. It so happened that I did have one, so I dropped it off that afternoon and that was the last I was going to see of Clive Mundy for almost five years.

We noticed his absence after the Bowdens got back. We thought that maybe they'd sent Clive back to Christchurch to do some work on their guest house but that wasn't it. Clive had simply left and James Bowden didn't like it. He wasn't going to get anybody else to do half the work that Clive had been doing for twice the money and he knew it. He got real nasty about it too — told everybody in the district that Clive was an ex-con who'd done a three-year stretch, who hadn't been able to get a job anywhere because of his record and that it was only out of Christian charity that he had employed Clive in the first place.

Bowden was really sounding off and would have kept bad-mouthing Clive except Ted shut him up with a few home truths.

'Another word out of you, Bowden, and I'll drop you where you stand,' Ted warned. 'For your information Clive Mundy was well liked and respected round here which is more than what can be said for you. If Clive did make a mistake and do time like you say he did, then it was long ago and he's paid his dues. As for him having a hard time getting a job, let me tell you something: any one of a dozen cockies in this valley, me included, would have given Clive a job like a shot. His prison record wouldn't have made any difference.'

I don't think any of us had ever seen Ted so angry about anything before. If Bowden had been silly enough to make some smart-mouth remark, Ted would have hung one on him for sure. But it didn't come to that. Bowden just mumbled something about having a right to his opinion and sloped off.

As the weeks went by we wondered about Clive, where he was and what he was doing, and I was just a little bit hurt that he hadn't written or tried to get in touch. Sammy Mita got it into his head that the Bowdens had murdered old Clive and buried him in their vegie garden but I didn't put too much stock in that. 'The Bowdens wouldn't do anything unless there was a profit in it, Sammy,' I said. But Sammy wasn't convinced and within days the rumour was all over the district. We even had a visit from the police — talk about embarrassing. They questioned most of us and spent some time with the Bowdens but nothing came of it, thank God. If they'd started digging up the vegie garden we would never have lived it down.

The due date for the grand opening of Bowden's hunting lodge came and went without anything happening so we thought maybe Bowden hadn't been able to get everything finished without Clive's help. It seemed reasonable enough but just to complicate matters Bowden called round to see Frank Avery and made him an offer to buy his property. According to Frank, Bowden was real keen to buy even though he was trying hard not to show it. Without quibbling he offered him 10 percent over government valuation. Frank had been trying to sell his property for the last two years but because it wasn't worth much he would never have got enough for it to start again anywhere else. Even with Bowden's offer of 10 percent over government valuation it still wasn't enough and as Bowden seemed keen and Frank didn't owe him any favours he decided to hold out for more.

A week later Bowden bumped his offer up to 15 percent over government valuation but Frank told him he wouldn't accept anything less than 35 percent. For a while Bowden kept his distance and it looked as though Frank had overplayed his hand but two weeks later Bowden agreed to Frank's terms. 'That bastard's up to something,' was Ted's opinion, and most of us shared it.

Bowden maintained that he only wanted Frank's property so he could expand the hunting area for his prospective clients, but that didn't add up and you didn't need a degree in economics to work it out. Bowden had already got himself deep in debt borrowing against his property in Christchurch to build his flash new house along with the cabins and generally get things ready. Now he'd gone and borrowed against his lodge, which wasn't even operating yet, to buy Frank's property at 35 percent over government valuation.

For Bowden to make enough money to pay off what he owed he was going to need something like a daily intake of 50 high-paying clients for all 365 days of the year. It just wasn't feasible. He had to be up to something. He was acting too damn confident not to be. After everything was signed up Frank took off and bought a place just outside of Raetihi. He's still there today, living in retirement after handing the reins over to his son.

Just days after Frank had moved out Bowden had some visitors turn up in flash cars wearing suits and smelling of money. We thought maybe they were his first clients but they only stayed for a couple of hours then left. They all seemed very happy about something and there was a lot of handshaking going on which made us more curious than ever. Things got almost too much for us over the following weeks. Bowden still wasn't getting any clients yet he was still smiling. But things were about to change.

It was only when the police paid us another visit we realised the Bowdens hadn't been around their place for almost two weeks. We thought maybe they were in Christchurch again, but they weren't. The police wouldn't tell us anything except that they were 'very anxious to speak to Mr Bowden' and they would appreciate any information concerning his whereabouts. Whatever it was the police were after Bowden for, none of us had a clue, but Sammy started his rumour going again and some of the boys actually went over to Bowden's place and dug up the vegie garden. It was all done under the cover of darkness and they didn't find any bodies, but Len Utley, who wasn't noted for his intelligence, fell into the septic tank which livened things up a bit.

Almost a month went by before we heard anything else about James Bowden. He'd been arrested in Australia and deported back to New Zealand to face charges of fraud. All his property had been seized and sold to pay off his debts but he still owed thousands. At his trial he was convicted and sent down for seven years. All the legal stuff was handled in Christchurch so we didn't get too much in the way of details, which hacked us off a bit. Even Ted, with his influential friends in all the right places, couldn't find out any more than what we already knew, so we had to be satisfied with what we had, even though we weren't.

Four years and ten months later I finished my carpentry apprenticeship and took off for a week's holiday to the Bay of Islands to celebrate. The James Bowden affair had been all but forgotten and I was going to catch a marlin, or at least try to. The journey took me twice as long as it would today and Paihia was about half the size it is now. There were a few charter boats operating and according to the locals they were all good, but if I hadn't done much big game fishing then the man to see was Captain Jack, who had a boat called the *Blue Lady*.

I had no trouble finding the *Blue Lady* or Captain Jack. He was elderly but fit looking and tanned and wore a sailor's cap and a silvery grey beard, smoked a pipe and five years before, he'd been known as Clive Mundy.

We shook hands and acted as though meeting up like that was the most natural thing in the world. Then we went below decks and in keeping with the traditions of the sea, Clive opened a bottle of rum. We talked about old times and it was only natural that James Bowden came into the conversation. 'You might have heard about him being convicted of fraud and copping a seven-year stretch,' I said, and Clive smiled.

'I must be slipping. The way I had it planned, he should have got at least ten.'

I couldn't think of anything to say to that but I didn't have to. After pouring himself another rum and pushing the bottle across the table towards me, Clive started on a story that had its beginnings way back in 1918.

'It was just after the end of the First World War,' Clive began. 'Bob Eamon, Simon Bowden, that is James's stepfather, and I had come back from France and even for war heroes, jobs were as scarce as hens' teeth. But Bob got a position managing a cattle station down Otago way and because we'd been mates all through the war he soon got us on the payroll as well. He also got himself married.

'For the most part the job consisted of rounding up cattle which strayed into the high country and there was quite a bit of that because the fences weren't up to much — something to do with the war shortage. We worked long hours in freezing conditions for days at a time, camping out, and the pay wasn't all that great, so when I saw a chance to make a bit extra I took it.

'I noticed in our first couple of musters that some of the stock from the neighbouring properties had got mixed up with ours. There was nothing wrong with that; it happened all the time in the high country. The correct procedure was to separate your neighbour's cattle from yours and put them in the road paddock to be picked up, but I figured out a more profitable way to get rid of them and Simon didn't need much persuasion to come in on the deal.

'It was only a small operation at first. We'd herd a few head down-river to the stockyards and find a buyer who wasn't going to ask too many questions and everything would be sweet, but we got greedy. Before long we were spending more time rounding up cattle off the neighbouring properties than we were our own. We even set up cattle traps in the bush, just like the ones I showed you young blokes how to make. Anyway, we got caught and Simon Bowden, being the bastard he was, turned King's evidence to get immunity from prosecution and because he wanted Bob out of the way on account of him and Bob's missus having an affair, he implicated Bob as well.

'He told the police that it was all Bob's idea. Of course Bob had never had anything to do with any of it but they didn't believe him. We both got sent down for three years and Simon did a runner with Bob's wife. While we were inside Bob earned a bit more remission than I did and got released a month before me. As soon as I got out I went looking for him but it was like Bob had vanished into thin air. I couldn't find any trace of him.

'About three years later I heard through the grapevine that his wife had divorced him and married Simon and that she had a son. As far as I was concerned Bob was better off without her but I still wanted to find Bob. It wasn't easy travelling around like that with jobs being so scarce and everything. I ended up on the West Coast where I'd heard there was a bit of work to be done on the fishing boats, but there wasn't. Things were just as bad there as anywhere else. But my luck changed almost straight away.

'I met up with an old prospector called Luke — I can't remember his other name. He'd been panning for gold for so long he had webbed feet, he reckoned. We camped in a hut alongside the river and lived on the trout we caught in our fish traps and wood pigeons that we snared in the bush. It was rough but we were getting gold, lots of it. Luke claimed he'd never seen anything like it in his 50 years of prospecting. Inside of a year we'd made a fortune.

'Luke carried on prospecting because he reckoned he was too old to change, while I headed for Christchurch and bought half shares in a pub. For the next twenty years life was good. The only damper on things was not being able to find my old mate to share my good fortune with. Then one day, who should walk into the pub but Simon Bowden himself.

'I'd sworn to murder the bastard for what he had done, but one look at him and I knew that fate had dealt to him far worse than what I could ever have done. He was a sick man, riddled with cancer, and had come to settle accounts. He said he was sorry for what he had done and wanted to put the record straight by writing out a full confession that would exonerate Bob, but he made one condition. The confession wasn't to be sent to the Department of Justice until after his death, which he said wasn't too far away, and going by the looks of him you could believe it.

'True to his word he wrote out a confession and gave it to James with instructions for it to be sent to the authorities after his death, which occurred two years later. I waited until after the funeral then went round to see James who by that time had got married and had changed his name officially to Bowden. I reminded him about the letter of confession and he said he'd send it to the authorities provided I did a small favour first.

'I didn't like the sound of that, but said I'd listen. He explained how he had the opportunity of a lifetime to buy a guest house right in the middle of the city but he needed a loan. He insisted it was just a loan and that he'd pay me back as soon as his mother got back from Europe. Apparently she was of German heritage and as soon as the war was over, the Second World War that is, she'd gone over with her parents to meet her grandparents who she'd never seen, and to claim an inheritance which according to Bowden was nothing short of a fortune. The only snag was he needed the money straight away and couldn't wait for his mother to return from Europe.

'It all sounded on the level and above board and as I wanted Bob's name cleared more than anything else I agreed. I sold my half of the pub to my partner on the proviso that I could buy it back at the same price within twelve months and handed the money over to Bowden. In the meantime I just waited around for Bowden's mother to come back from Europe, which she did three months later. Surprisingly enough Bowden paid me back and I wasted no time in buying back my half of the pub, but then everything started going wrong.

'That very night the pub caught fire and burnt to the ground and my partner hadn't renewed the insurance. He had tried, but had been unable to secure any insurance because of a five-year stretch he'd done in Mt Eden. I hadn't known about this at the time. He blamed himself for everything and promised to make it up to me one day but there was nothing either of us could do.

'We were both broke and owed quite a bit of money to the breweries for the stock that had been lost in the fire. My partner cleared off and I went to work for the Bowdens. There wasn't much else I could do. I had a prison record as well and people aren't too keen to employ an ex-con. Working for the Bowdens was about as pleasant as having a tooth pulled but I stuck it out in the hope that one day Bob would get in touch with his son and I would be able to tell him the good news about having his name cleared.

'Well, as we both know, Charger, that didn't happen. Bob died and Bowden inherited his father's property. I was ready to chuck it in after that and tell the Bowdens what they could do with their job but I thought I'd take a look at the place where my old mate had spent the last twenty years of his life. I had to admit, I fell in love with the valley straight off. I was even thinking of sticking around until that day you, Sammy and Ted came over to help me shift all that furniture. When you and Sammy dropped that chest and all those papers were blowing around the first piece I picked up was the handwritten confession from Simon Bowden which exonerated Bob. I couldn't understand it. James Bowden had vowed and declared he'd sent it to the authorities, so after you and the boys left I did a bit of investigating.

'I went through all the paperwork in that chest and found a letter written to Bowden from his mother. She was living the high life off her inheritance in Sydney, Australia and she still had the knife out for Bob. She threatened to cut Bowden out of her will if he ever sent the confession off to the authorities and of course Bowden had complied with his mother's wishes. Let me tell you, Charger, I was an angry man that day, angrier than I've ever been in my life. That bastard Bowden had let his father go to his grave a convicted felon, just for the sake of money, and the irony is Bowden's mother didn't have any money — she'd lost it all on some mining property that went bust.

'I figured if Bowden was so fond of gold I'd give him some. I'd give him plenty. What he didn't know was when he had Bob's old home demolished I'd rescued an old wooden box that Bob had used as a kind of filing cabinet. It contained some old diaries and personal papers but there was still plenty of room, so I added a few things. I had a small jar of gold dust left over from my days on the West Coast which I'd been keeping as a souvenir more than anything else and that was the first thing to go into the box. Then I added some diary notes and some very official-looking reports from the Lands and Survey Department. And that old map you lent me — I drew some very suggestive circles on some of the landmarks that took in Bowden's property and that of Frank Avery.

'When it was all put together the effect was magic and the end result inevitable. Because of what I'd put in that old box — the additions to the diary, the jar of gold, the Lands and Survey reports, the assayer's assessment, the landmarks on the map — Bowden was convinced that he was sitting on a goldmine and he acted true to form. I just wish I'd been there to see it. The markings on the map had him convinced that there was a lot of gold on Frank's property too. That's why he was so keen to buy the place. But of course he needed money to do that, so he sold shares to some speculators from Auckland, just like I knew he would. Once they found out the whole thing was a scam, they prosecuted just like I knew they would, and the rest is history.'

Clive helped himself to another small nip of rum and I helped myself to a big one. I needed it. 'Just clear up a couple of points for me, Clive,' I asked. 'This boat of yours must have set you back a fair bit and you weren't exactly rich the last time I saw you and those diary notes you mentioned, along with the official reports from the Lands and Survey Department — where did you get those from at such short notice?'

Clive leaned back and smiled. 'Well I've got Frank Avery to thank for all this. You could say he paid me a commission for arranging the very profitable sale of his property. As for all the fancy paperwork and diary notes, Frank did that as well. The markings on the map were exceptionally good. You see, Charger, Frank had done time for forgery many years ago and although he'd stayed inside the law after serving his sentence he'd never lost his touch. He was one of the best in his day you know. He was quite happy to work for me. He wanted to put things right, to settle accounts you might say, for old times' sake. Good bloke is Frank. He'd never forgiven himself since burning our pub down.'

CHAPTER 3

A Fortunate Handicap

I was just 16 years old when Claude Dupree first came to the Wanganui River Valley, yet I can remember it as if it were yesterday. It was late summer 1946. Japan had formally surrendered six months before, bringing the Second World War to an end and there was still something of a festive feeling in the atmosphere. Wool prices had gone through the roof, there was plenty of work about and people were going about their everyday business with a positive outlook for the future.

Nobody in the valley could actually remember Claude arriving, so he must have snuck in when nobody was looking — or maybe we were all out for the day. But he was there all right. Camped down at the river using an old railway tarp for a tent. It was obvious right from the start that Claude wasn't from our part of the world because of his accent. We thought he was from America but he soon put us straight on that. He was from Edmonton in Canada. What wasn't obvious was Claude's handicap, if that's the right word.

He'd lost his left arm just below the elbow and his left leg just below the knee at the Battle of Dieppe where things hadn't gone too well for our side. His artificial arm and leg were made from aluminium and shaped to look like the real thing and because of the natural way he moved about his encumbrance just wasn't that noticeable. He didn't even bother to limp except when he was tired, and that didn't happen too often. I got to know Claude better than anybody in those first few weeks, calling in on him after work most evenings and weekends.

He told me about his life in Canada before the war. On leaving school he'd taken on an apprenticeship as a blacksmith, but after two years at the forge he'd had enough and headed off for the Rocky Mountains. It was quite a rugged experience for a young bloke, but he reckoned his Sioux Indian ancestry stood him in good stead. His parents were of French and Scottish extraction, but his grandfather, who had the given name of Talks-To-His-Horses, had been renowned as a great hunter in the tribe and had taken part in the battle of the Little Bighorn where General Custer and the Seventh Cavalry came second.

Claude had carved out a living for himself in the Rockies as a trapper and he'd hunted bear and elk and even built himself a log cabin to live in. It was nothing for him to spend anything up to six months at a time in the mountains, only coming out as far as the Pine Bluff trading post to sell his furs and stock up on supplies before heading straight back to the high country and the life he loved.

He knew very little about what was going on in the world and cared even less. His world hadn't changed much since the days of Boone and Crockett and it suited him down to the snow-covered ground he walked on. The war had been going for almost a year before he found out about it. He smiled whilst recalling the day he'd called in at the trading post and read an old newspaper.

'If I'd had enough flour and coffee to see me through another winter I would never have gone to the damn store in the first place. Might have missed the war altogether, but for that. Would definitely have missed out on Dieppe and wouldn't have had to make do with this,' he laughed, tapping his artificial leg with a stick of manuka.

You had to hand it to Claude; life had dealt him a cruel blow but he wasn't about to let it get him down or rob him of his sense of humour. Though to be candid, I thought he might have been bucking the odds a bit when he told me he was going to spend the coming winter trapping possums.

'I know this isn't the Rockies, mate,' I told him with a sweeping gesture that took in the whole western side of the valley, 'but there's some pretty rugged country out there, and our winters can't be taken too lightly either.'

Claude thanked me for my concern, but said he'd like to give it a try anyway, and he did. As soon as the first chills of autumn hit us, Claude took to the bush with just a few things in a small pack, an axe and a cut down .303 rifle. It didn't look like much for a bloke taking on his first New Zealand winter, and it wasn't much. He didn't even have any traps as far as I could tell, and I couldn't help harbouring some fears for his safety.

Months went by without any of us hearing anything. We had one hell of a winter that year too, and all kinds of rumours started circulating regarding Claude's whereabouts. He'd died of exposure, he'd met with an accident, he was on the run from the police, doing a stretch in Mt Eden; everybody had a theory. My old man was of the opinion that Claude had simply found the going too tough and had quietly left the valley. 'There's no way a bloke can set himself up in the bush when he's only got one good arm and leg,' he said, and our neighbour, Ted Thompson, backed him up on that.

'You're not wrong there, John,' he agreed. 'It's a tough game that possum trapping, even for a fit bloke with all his parts.'

I was about the only one who believed that Claude was out there somewhere, working his line and living off whatever he could trap, shoot or catch, but I didn't say anything. Looking back with the benefit of hindsight, I should have done, because it turned out I was right, and would have had something to feel smug about.

Spring had finally arrived and I was giving my new finding dog, Scout, a run near the headwaters of Thunder Creek. The bloke I'd bought him off had warned me that Scout was a 'long range finder'. I wasn't too sure what that meant at the time and as I'd been skiting about how experienced I was, thought it best not to ask. I was finding out though.

Scout was taking me further afield than I'd ever been before. Being up among the tall timber can be quite intimidating for a young joker who's never been past the scrub-covered foothills and river flats. After four hours of steady tramping I was starting to see parts of the valley that I didn't even know existed. Finally Scout bailed up a crusty old boar in a wet patch of fern that backed up onto a sandstone bluff. He seemed quite pleased with himself but it took a fair amount of gentle encouragement followed by firm inducement and screaming abuse before he'd go in for the hold. The boar wasn't much use for anything except dog tucker and I wasn't too sure if the one I had was worth feeding, but I lifted it onto my back anyway and looked around for the quickest way out of there.

The weather was starting to take a turn for the worse and I was only lightly clad in a pair of ex-army trousers and a football jersey, the accepted national dress for all pighunters back then. Hats were seldom worn and hobnail boots were, almost without exception.

There was a spur leading off the bluff that went in the right direction, so I followed it for about quarter of an hour before dropping down to the creek, which opened up into a gentle-flowing stream with wide grassy banks. It reminded me of a picture postcard I'd seen once, and I could smell woodsmoke. Claude's camp was just a few minutes downstream. He was pouring out two mugs of tea as I showed up, like he was expecting me, which he was. 'Heard you growling at your dog up by the bluffs,' he said.

I felt really embarrassed hearing him say that, because Claude neither used nor approved of coarse language, and I'd been swearing something awful at Scout. 'A lot of people have given you up for dead,' I said hastily, changing the subject.

'It's not the first time that's happened,' he smiled, 'and chances are it won't be the last. I kind of lose track of time when I'm in the woods.'

I liked the way he called the bush the 'woods', and I liked his camp too, a real neat set-up. He'd built a hut with roof and walls clad with totara shingles and a stone and ponga chimney. It looked more like a cottage than a hut. His skin shelter and work area was made up from white pine framing and the canvas tarp he'd used for a tent when camped down by the river. All told he had over a thousand first grade skins ready for the auction, all taken with snares made from Bowden wire.

He reckoned he might have got a few more if he'd had some proper traps. Cripes, I believed it. He even had a vegie garden with caulis and cabbages that he'd grown from seeds. For all intents and purposes, Claude Dupree was totally self-sufficient. I would have liked to stay, but my folks, being the over-protective type, were likely to panic if I didn't get home by dark. So after another brew I headed out, following Claude's trap line which led to a patch of second growth overlooking Ted Thompson's lambing paddock. I was just five minutes from home.

Next day I retraced my steps with Ted Thompson's pack horse, Samson, to help Claude bring his skins out. He got a good price for them from a buyer in Wanganui, opened a savings account with the Post Office, bought himself a hundred secondhand traps from a bloke in Ridgeway Street, then headed back to the bush, as if being in town was about the worst thing he'd ever experienced. Maybe it was.

Prices for summer skins weren't too bad that year, so Claude said he'd carry on as usual. I spent every day of the holidays with him that summer and learnt that no matter how different something might be at first, spend enough time with it and you get to the stage where you hardly notice it. Like driving a new car where all the controls are on the opposite side of what you're used to.

Claude did things differently because of the way he was fixed. So it was only natural that he did things the way he did, which looked so unnatural you couldn't help but notice. Like the way he held the box in the crook of his elbow when striking a match to light the fire, or the way he walked sideways when going up and down a steep bit of country. There were lots of other things too, but after a while I didn't really notice them any more, mostly because they didn't really matter.

Whatever Claude was doing, he invariably got it done and the final result was always good. I can't think of anything he couldn't do, apart from run, which prevented him from pighunting in the accepted manner, with dogs. But if he wanted a bit of wild pork for the pot he'd just sneak along the bush edge in the early mornings and bowl one over with his .303.

An incident during the following roar showed me just how versatile and skilled Claude was. We were sidling around a bluff on a narrow ledge some three hundred feet above Tennant's Creek trying to close in on a roaring fallow buck when Claude missed his footing. It was a close thing. He all but went tumbling into the gorge below, only just managing to grab hold of something with his good hand in time to arrest his fall. It gave me a hell of a fright; I almost gave birth.

Somehow Claude's artificial leg came loose and we were too busy hanging on to do anything but watch as it slid off the ledge and bounced on a rock before making a long spiralling descent to the flooding, muddy waters of the creek below. Had it been anything but an artificial leg it might have looked graceful, but as it was, grotesque would be a more fitting description of the spectacle.

Somehow we got off that ledge and made it back to camp, with Claude using a length of manuka lashed to his rifle for a crutch. 'How long before you can get another leg, Claude?' I asked him back at his hut, while hanging the billy over the fire.

'Too damn long if I go through the usual channels,' he answered, 'but if I can get access to a forge and some tools and especially if I could get hold of some er-loo-min-um, I think maybe I could make one.'

I knew Gus Polanski, our local farrier, wouldn't have any objection to letting Claude use his forge and tools, but I wasn't too sure about the er-loo-min-um. It wasn't that I couldn't lay my hands on any, it was just that I didn't know what Claude was talking about. If he'd said aluminium, it would have been fine, but he kept calling it er-loo-min-um. We wasted the best part of an hour discussing the stuff before I finally caught on.

Before leaving that afternoon, I made sure Claude had everything within easy reach and made the return journey next morning with Samson. Claude reckoned that Samson wasn't the most comfortable horse he'd ever ridden, but said it was a whole lot easier than walking with an improvised crutch. Back at my place I borrowed the old man's Chevy and raced Claude out to meet Gus. They'd already met briefly when Claude first came to the valley, but I re-introduced them anyway. Gus's daughter, Helen, was there too, and her and Claude hit it off straight away. The attraction was both instant and mutual — anybody could see that. Helen remembered something and ran back into the house and came back out again a few minutes later with a pair of crutches that her father had used a few months back when he'd broken his ankle.

Claude said something about having to make a start so I raced into town to see a mate whose father had a scrap metal yard. As for Claude's er-loo-min-um, there wasn't a whole lot to be had, but we managed to scrape together a sugar sack full, which I thought would be plenty, and paid a quid for it, which I thought was more than plenty. As soon as I got back, Claude started melting down the scraps of aluminium in a big iron pot. Then he got me to one side and asked me to take my boot and sock off my left foot, and roll up my trouser leg. I wondered what the hell, but did it anyway.

Helen came out giggling, carrying a bucket of plaster of Paris and an armful of bandages that looked as if they'd been ripped up from an old bedsheet. Before I knew what was happening, Claude and Helen were bandaging my left leg and foot with the linen strips soaked in the plaster of Paris mix. It took them about twenty minutes to do the job and I had to wait for about that long again for it to go hard.

Using a pair of tin snips, Claude removed the cast in two equal halves. I was starting to get the idea. He now had a perfect mould of a lower left leg and foot and I didn't have any hairs left on my lower left leg and foot. Ask anybody who's had a plaster cast removed and they'll tell you what it's like. The two halves of the mould had to be bound together again, before Claude put it in a bucket and packed sand all around it. 'The sand will hold everything in place,' he explained.

Gus and I would have liked to help but Claude had everything under control, and as he was the only one who knew what he was doing we thought it best just to keep out of his way. As soon as the aluminium had melted, Claude poured it into the mould then poured water over the sand in the bucket to help speed up the cooling process.

It was a big moment when Claude broke open the mould to reveal his shiny new leg. We all stood around grinning at each other, not too sure of what to say. He spent the rest of the day putting finishing touches to his leg and attaching a kind of socket with some leather straps running off it. The only thing Claude didn't have or couldn't make right there and then was another boot, so Gus gave him one from an old pair he had lying around the place. Claude walked around on his new leg for a few minutes just to try it out. He seemed to be moving around just as good as ever. 'It's a little heavier than my old one,' he admitted. 'The commercially made ones are hollow, and so lighter, but this will do fine until I get a new one.'

Watching a one-armed man making himself an artificial leg was about the best example of self-reliance I'd ever seen. Gus thought so too, but Claude couldn't see what all the fuss was about. 'Take a look around,' he invited. 'Most everything you see is manmade: the homes we live in, the cars we drive, the clothes we wear, the plates we eat off, the cups we drink out of — they've all been made by somebody from somewhere. Why should it be any different for an artificial leg? Or for me making one, just because I happen to be missing a couple of parts? I'm a somebody from somewhere, just like you. I believe we are all capable of making just about anything if we really want to, if given the time and the will to apply ourselves.'

The simple truth behind Claude's philosophy wasn't lost on any of us, and if you thought it over it couldn't be argued with either. Helen was very impressed, and it wasn't too long after that that her and Claude started keeping company. He'd come out of the bush on Fridays and they'd spend the weekends going to the picture theatre in town, or picnicking on the river, or just walking along holding hands, the way courting couples used to do back then. This state of affairs between Helen and Claude lasted until Christmas then, for no apparent reason, stopped. Neither of them told anybody anything and the rest of us didn't ask any questions. It was none of our business anyway.

I called in to see Claude at his camp hoping to cheer him up a bit, and invited him to spend New Year's Eve with the Morrisons. He thanked me for the thought, but declined on the strength that he was moving camp. 'That's okay,' I said. 'I'll give you a hand.'

'You don't understand, Charger,' Claude explained. 'I'm not talking about moving an hour or so upriver; I'm heading for the West Coast of the South Island. I've heard plenty about it and I thought I'd go and take a look for myself.'

This bit of news just about floored me. We were supposed to be mates, and mates don't just up and leave like that. 'What the hell do you want to go up the West Coast for?' I demanded. 'It never stops raining down there. Even the sheep have webbed feet.'

I tried everything I could to talk Claude out of going, but his mind was made up. He promised to write, but more than a year passed before I received word from him. In a half-page letter he said that he was camped a half day's march up Bonnie Creek, which was situated some nine miles or so south of a small settlement called Haven. It was good hearing from Claude, but then I had to wait another seven months for my holidays before I could do anything about looking him up.

Finding the West Coast of the South Island wasn't too much of a problem, but nobody down there, it seemed, had ever heard of Haven, and I couldn't find it on the map. I was just about ready to give up and go home, and the truth is, if I hadn't taken a wrong turning twenty minutes out of Westport I would never have found the place. I don't think anybody else would have done either, including the people who lived there, all 24 of them.

Haven consisted of a general store with a single petrol bowser outside, a dozen or so dwellings and a pub, empty except for the publican, who didn't know where Bonnie Creek was. 'If you hang around till about five o'clock you'll catch the crowd. One of them will tell you where it is,' he promised.

At five o'clock the crowd, consisting of the owner of the general store and his brother, and a couple of fencing contractors, showed up, but none of them knew where Bonnie Creek was either, though they'd all heard of it and agreed it was around there somewhere. Half an hour later the crowd had swelled even more by one old bloke introduced as Lloyd, a retired fisherman, who never went anywhere, or cared to, but he knew where Bonnie Creek was.

'Just take the first turn to your right past the store, and follow your nose till you come to the bridge. That's Bonnie Creek,' he said. 'It's about a two-and-a-half-hour walk.'

'I'm driving,' I told him.

Lloyd thought about this for a moment. 'Fair enough, young fella,' he decided, 'but it still shouldn't take you any longer than two and a half hours.'

I made it to Bonnie Creek okay, but it was too late in the day to go hiking off after my mate so I slept in the truck and took off at first light next morning, reaching Claude's camp in time for morning tea. His hut was a dead ringer for the one he'd built back on the Wanganui River, except for the stone chimney. Claude welcomed me like a prodigal son, with slappings and hand shakings, a mug of hot tea and a plate of venison stew. 'The hunting's real good round here,' he said. 'Stick around long enough and you'll see for yourself.'

'Where's your skin shelter?' I asked through a mouthful of stew.

Claude smiled. 'I'm not trapping possums any more, Charger. I've found something a little more profitable. Come on and I'll show you.'

I followed Claude into his hut and from under his bunk he dragged out four preserving jars full of gold flakes and tiny nuggets. I didn't have a clue what it was worth, but it looked like a fortune. I was too stunned to say anything, but I noticed that there was another sleeping bag on the spare bunk. 'That belongs to my partner, Stuart,' Claude informed me. 'He's spending a few days in Greymouth catching up on a little business.'

Claude spent most of the day talking excitedly about how he and Stuart had found the gold quite by accident while possuming the previous winter. 'We did a little more panning and we were getting gold in almost every scoop,' he grinned. 'We've kind of speeded up the operation using riffle boxes, but we have to be careful because what we're doing isn't strictly legal. There's all kinds of licensing and regulations involved and I'm sure we've broken some, if not all of them. That's the reason for Stuart being in Greymouth — he's seeking legal advice with regards to our little operation.'

I stayed with Claude for the next three days doing nothing in particular except laze around camp and talk about old times. He admitted to being a little more broken up than what he'd let on when he and Helen had gone their separate ways, but reckoned it was all for the best. 'I'm only happy when I'm outdoors, Charger, and I think Helen was more suited to city life.'

Claude was right about that. About six months after he'd left the district, Helen had married some executive type from Auckland and by all accounts was as happy as a pig in a turnip patch, but I didn't say anything. 'By the way,' I asked, remembering the time at Gus Polanski's place, 'did you ever get another leg?'

'Sure did,' Claude smiled, lifting up his trouser leg to show me his new addition. 'Light as a feather and I can walk on it all day.'

Stuart showed up next day with a pack full of supplies and I heard him tell Claude that he got the paperwork 'fixed up'. I assumed he was referring to their licences and such. I didn't go much on Stuart, a real sleazy type, but he was Claude's mate, so I kept quiet. It was going to be a bit crowded with three of us in the hut so I headed for home that day. Claude seemed genuinely sorry to see me go, and once again promised to write. As I headed off downstream the grey, overcast sky matched my feelings. I couldn't shake off the feeling that I would never see Claude again, and although I wrote to him on several occasions care of the pub in Haven, I received no reply in the months that followed.

I figured he'd made his fortune, gone back to Canada and bought himself a hunting lodge. It had been his dream back in the old days on the Wanganui River, and he'd talked about it many times. Claude did in fact make his fortune, get back to Canada and buy his hunting lodge, but there was a bit more to it than that.

I got the full story later on that year at the national amateur boxing championships in Wellington. I'd been given a unanimous decision over Dave Balford, a middleweight from Palmerston North, on account he hadn't even shown up for the fight, but I decided to hang around anyway to watch the other bouts.

During the interval I was sneaking a smoke out in the foyer when a bloke came up and asked me if I'd ever managed to find my mate. He looked familiar but I couldn't place him and didn't know what he was talking about. 'I'm sure it was you,' he insisted. 'Weren't you looking for a mate camped up Bonnie Creek about a year or so back?'

Memory came flooding back. He was Frank somebody-or-other, one of the fencing contractors I'd met at the Haven pub. I told Frank that I'd caught up with Claude and that we'd spent a few days together. Frank nodded understandingly and said, 'So you wouldn't have been there when the big hoo-ha erupted between your mate and his partner?'

'No,' I said. 'What hoo-ha was that?'

Frank had a quick look over his shoulder to make sure no one was within earshot before continuing. 'Well, this mate of yours,' Frank explained, 'was doing a bit of prospecting without a licence up Bonnie Creek, with that partner of his, and they'd struck it rich. And your mate's partner, Stuart Pope I think his name was, did a runner with the gold, leaving your mate high and dry. Apparently this Stuart bloke headed into the bush and hid the gold with the intention of coming back for it when things had cooled down. But this mate of yours was quite a tracker by all accounts and had no trouble finding it and taking off into the bush himself. Being the mongrel he was, this Stuart character got the cops onto your mate, told the police that your mate had only been working for him and had stolen his gold. He even produced the licence that he'd had made out in his name only, to back up his story. The police put out a search for your mate but nothing came of it until about three months later when they caught up with him, right here in Wellington. He was about to board a ship bound for Canada. Of course, he denied all knowledge of any gold. The cops checked his bank account and all kinds of records to see if he'd made any deposits overseas, but they couldn't come up with anything. They went through his luggage with a fine-tooth comb, but didn't find anything there either. They had to let him go in the finish. I suppose the cops figured that your mate had taken the gold but had dumped it somewhere. What was your mate's name, anyway?' Frank asked as an afterthought.

'Claude Dupree,' I told him, 'and thanks for the story.'

Later on that night I thought about everything Frank had told me. And everything fitted. Stuart being a ratbag just as I thought he was, Claude being able to follow his tracks through the bush with the skills passed on by his Sioux ancestors, and hiding out in the bush and loving every minute of it. I had a pretty good idea how he got the gold out of the country too. My suspicions were confirmed just before Christmas that year. I got a letter from Claude with an Edmonton postmark on the envelope. There was a photograph of him standing outside a newly built residence with a sign saying Dupree's Hunting and Fishing Lodge. His letter read in part, 'You're welcome to stay any time, Charger, for as long as you like. And I hope you like the look of the place. You ought to. It cost me an arm and a leg.'

CHAPTER 4

Dog Control

When Miles Shortland had his pighunting days brought to a permanent halt by a very irate Captain Cooker nobody was too upset about it. He'd got ripped to the bone from ankle to thigh and the muscle damage was irreparable. Even after months of treatment and physiotherapy he could only manage a slow walk with a pronounced limp, for no more than a few minutes at a time and not without considerable pain.

But as already stated, nobody was feeling sorry for him. In fact the only regret heard from those who cared to voice their opinion was for the boar not finishing the job. 'Would've saved the taxpayer a packet in hospital expenses if it had done,' Bob Proctor was heard to comment one afternoon at the Riverside Tavern.

Miles Shortland had moved into the district with his wife and eight-year-old son three years before, and within a week of settling in got on the wrong side of Jim Clayton, his neighbour. Jim had been training a couple of huntaway pups and had them shaping up nicely. It was Jim's practice to let them off the chain for half an hour or so, to burn off any extra energy before putting them through their paces. That way they'd quieten down quicker and be easier to command. It's a common enough practice when training young dogs for whatever purposes.

On this occasion though, they just happened to be off the chain and crossed over the boundary onto the property of one Miles Shortland, and without hesitation Miles Shortland shot them both dead. It was uncalled for and totally unnecessary, but Miles claimed he was within his rights. 'Those dogs of yours were running loose and unsupervised on my property, thereby constituting a danger to my sheep. The law's on my side,' he told Jim as though he'd done the district a favour by ridding it of two wild and rabid sheep killers.

Technically speaking Miles did have the law on his side but that didn't mean he had to do what he did. The dogs hadn't been anywhere near his sheep and even if they had been it's highly debatable, trained as they were, that they would have constituted any danger.

Not long after that, Miles upset his other neighbour, Bob Proctor, along with everybody associated with the Pony Club. Miles discovered that the section of Bob's road paddock that had been used by the Pony Club for as long as anyone could remember crossed over into his side of the boundary. The amount of ground in question wouldn't have been more than a quarter of an acre. It meant a lot to the Pony Club because of the way they had their jumps arranged. The correct distance between each jump along with the overall distance of the circuit was very important and had been carefully set out.

The sacrifice of a quarter of an acre wouldn't have made any difference to Miles, but that didn't stop him. He told Bob to shift the boundary back to where it should be within 30 days, or be taken to court. Bob and the Pony Club had no choice but to comply. Within a very short time the rest of us good people of the Wanganui River district had come to the inescapable conclusion that Miles Shortland was a ratbag of the first order whose only purpose in life was to make the lives of others as miserable as possible, for no other reason than he derived some kind of sick pleasure out of it.

We all did our best to keep clear of the bloke, which wasn't hard to do. The real victims were his wife Mary and son Mark. They were the only ones ever seen actually working on the place, though slaving would be a more accurate word to use. From the time young Mark got off the school bus Miles would have him hard at it till it was too dark to see. And not just jobs you would normally associate with an eight-year-old either, like picking up the eggs from the hen house or feeding out scraps to the pigs. Miles had the kid digging post-holes and drains and filling in the pot-holes in the drive with gravel that he'd carried up from the creek a bucketload at a time.

As for Mary, in addition to being wife and mother, she had a few other jobs to keep herself occupied, like fencing, feeding out, haymaking, crutching, dipping, lambing, docking and doubling up as chief mechanic to keep their fading Ferguson operable and their pre-war model Dodge roadworthy. For his part, Miles went pighunting most every day. Jack Philburn reckoned that Miles Shortland couldn't be all bad if he was a pighunter, but that bit of homespun philosophy didn't cut any ice with me.

Pighunters can be low-life mongrels just like anyone else, and Miles Shortland was living proof of that. He had a four-dog pack which were fed only just enough to keep them alive and received nothing in the way of care or attention. If they got sick or injured then they either recovered or died. Miles couldn't have cared less. 'There's plenty of replacements at the pound,' was his attitude.

Mary would give the dogs a bit of extra tucker when Miles wasn't around, but she was always careful not to get caught. There would have been hell to pay otherwise. Though whether that would have stopped her or not is debatable. Mary had a thing for dogs; something special. She had one of her own, a black lab called Bo, which she'd trained as a gun dog retriever. God knows when she found the time. Occasionally we'd have gun dog trials arranged through the rod and gun club and Mary would come along and put Bo through the course. Watching Mary work her dog was an experience by itself. She never used verbal commands; all directions were given through a series of hand signals, thigh slappings and finger snapping.

She had Bo searching and finding, moving to the left or right or forward, and retrieving without a word passing her lips. It was more than impressive, it was uncanny. 'What's behind the hand signals, Mary?' I asked, intrigued by it all.

'Bo is a hunting dog, Charger,' Mary explained. 'Verbal commands in the field carry a long way and alert game.'

I could see the logic in what Mary was saying. 'It's a pity your training methods can't be used on pig dogs.'

Mary gave me a look as if I had a blank space between my ears. 'It works on pig dogs or any other kind of dogs, Charger,' she assured me. 'It's just a matter of teaching the dog to relate certain sounds to certain actions.'

I would have liked to spend longer talking training methods with Mary, but she was pushed for time. Mary was always pushed for time. Word about her and her dog got around the district faster than the gossip generated by an illicit affair. She was the main topic of conversation down at the club. There was even a motion put forward that she be given full membership and elected as official dog trainer and paid for her services.

Mary was flattered by all the attention and it was good to see her having something to smile about. Mark was happy too and real proud of his mum, which was more than could be said for Miles. We really hadn't done Mary any favours. Miles was seething with jealousy and making life even more unbearable for her and Mark.

Just how unbearable we had no way of knowing, but about six

weeks after Mary's last appearance at the gun dog trials we were to find out. I was on my way into town to pick up a few hardware items when I noticed the Shortlands' Dodge parked at the side of the road with the bonnet up. On hearing my approach, Mary stepped out onto the road and began to frantically wave me down.

She was in a hell of a state, crying so hard as to be barely coherent. 'It's Bo, Charger,' she sobbed. 'He's been shot. I've got to get him to the vet's. The fuel line on the Dodge is ruptured.'

Mary cradled Bo in her arms as I kept the Ford's accelerator flat to the floor all the way out to the veterinary clinic at the far end of town. While the vet worked on Bo, Mary and I sat in the waiting room and she told me that Miles had shot Bo, claiming that he had attacked his sheep.

Mary didn't believe it, and frankly neither did I. Miles Shortland was just doing what he did best, carrying out an act of sheer bastardy to cause somebody grief. As the time ticked by I got increasingly hopeful. It stood to reason that Bo had to have a fighting chance of recovery otherwise the vet wouldn't have been spending so much time on him. It was only an opinion, so I thought it best not to say anything to Mary. Just as well I didn't.

When the vet stepped into the waiting room the look on his face indicated anything but good news. 'I'm sorry, Mrs Shortland. We did everything we could but — '

We drove back in silence. I couldn't think of anything useful to say and Mary didn't feel like talking. I dropped her off at the gate and told her not to worry about her car, that I'd get somebody to replace the fuel line and bring it round later. Mary thanked me and as I watched her walk up to the house, my heart really grieved for the woman.

She'd only had two things in life to be thankful for, and now one of those had been taken from her. The whole district felt for Mary:

she'd taken the loss of Bo really hard. Word got round that she was spending more time with Miles's pig dogs, which we supposed was her way of compensating for not having a dog of her own.

She didn't seem to care if Miles knew about it either. We had no way of knowing whether it was true or not, but there was another rumour floating around that Mary hadn't spoken a single word to Miles since he'd shot Bo. I wasn't willing to believe that entirely because according to Jim Clayton, Mary and Mark had been pighunting with Miles. This was unusual because he'd never have bothered inviting them in the past. Most of us concluded that Miles was just trying to get back into Mary's favour, though Ted Thompson had a less charitable view. 'He's only taking her along to carry the pork, the lazy bastard.'

Whatever the reason it did at least give Mary a chance to get away from the farm. She might have even got round to getting a pack of her own together at some time and becoming a pighunter in her own right, if it hadn't been for the accident. Luckily for Miles, Jim Clayton had been out on horseback looking for strays that day. He'd heard the commotion from the dogs and gone over to investigate, arriving just moments before the boar broke free of the dogs. Jim didn't owe Miles any favours, but he loaded him onto his horse, got him back to the farm and from there drove him to the hospital in record time.

If Jim hadn't been on hand then there's every chance that Miles would have bled to death, but Jim never got any thanks for his efforts. While Miles was laid up in hospital there was some concern for Mary and Mark trying to run things on their own, but we needn't have worried. They managed quite nicely, thank you very much.

For all the use Miles had been around the place, they had, in effect, been operating on their own anyway. If anything, they seemed a whole lot happier without him. Mary started putting in more appearances at the gun dog trials and Mark had time to play football and all the other things that kids his age like to do. After being discharged from hospital, Miles stayed at his brother's place in town to save him travelling backwards and forwards every day for his physio treatment.

He put in the occasional appearance back at the farm but never stayed long. Finally he left for somewhere over on the East Coast where he had a few relatives. Then we heard that he'd blown his brains through the ceiling with his own hunting rifle, the one he'd used on Jim Clayton's dogs and Bo. As tragic a case as Miles Shortland had become, we still couldn't work up any sympathy for him. Even Mary and Mark seemed unaffected by his death.

They carried on as if nothing had happened, running the place on their own, hiring outside help only for the shearing. With Mary's Dodge spending more time up on the blocks than on the road, I called in one day to see if she wanted anything from town. She was down in the holding paddock giving the dogs a run, or at least that's what it looked like at first. After watching for a few minutes I realised she was putting them through a training schedule, using the same non-verbal methods she had at the gun dog trials.

Mark was standing by the fence watching with interest. 'G'day, Mark, how's things?'

Mark turned around and put his finger to his lips and said, 'Shssh. Mum's training the dogs.'

'Yeah, I can see that mate, but does that mean you have to be quiet?'

Mark nodded solemnly. 'Mum uses secret signs when she's training the dogs.'

He was doing his best to sound very serious. I felt sure Mary wouldn't mind me being there, but thought I'd play along with

Mark. 'D'you think I ought to leave, mate,' I suggested, 'before I find out any secrets?'

Mark looked up at me, smiling. 'Bet you can't work out what Mum's signals are for, Mr Morrison,' he said.

'Bet you two bob I can.'

'You're on, Mr Morrison.'

We shook hands. I stood there watching Mary put the dogs through a series of controlled runs and worked out that a single snap of the fingers was for the dogs to stop, two meant that they moved left, and three, right. Mark confirmed that this was so and looked worried at the prospect of losing two bob.

A slap on the thigh had the dogs coming to heel, then Mary sent Skipper the finding dog away with an underarm motion as though she was playing bowls. 'Mum's got a pig skin hidden in the bushes,' Mark confided. 'You watch what happens when Skipper finds it.'

Skipper was moving forward with his nose to the ground, searching through the patches of gorse. On finding the skin he started barking, then Bully and Rip, the two holders, took off. Once on the scene they grabbed hold of the skin. It was all very impressive and I couldn't help thinking that Mary's method of 'silent' command would have to give the hunter a considerable advantage in the field.

Bully and Rip were playing tug-o'-war with the skin, then Mary walked into view and clapped her hands together softly. 'Now she's telling them what good dogs they are,' I said to Mark, who looked up, grinning wider than ever.

'You're wrong, Mr Morrison, and you owe me two bob,' he answered, holding his hand out for the agreed sum. I dug a two shilling piece out of my hip pocket and handed it over. 'When Mum claps her hands together like that, it's a signal for the dogs to let go,' Mark explained. 'We use that when the dogs grab a sow with a litter, because Mum reckons we shouldn't kill sows with litters.'

'Quite right too, mate,' I agreed.

Mary spotted me about then, and after putting the dogs away came over, apologising for keeping me waiting.

'No problem, Mary, I was enjoying the show.'

Mary smiled modestly. 'It gave me something to do after I lost Bo.'

There was still a touch of sadness in her voice.

'D'you need anything from town, Mary?' I asked, purposely changing the subject.

Mary gave a quick shake of her head. 'I don't need anything from town, Charger, but I'd like you to take a look at my car shed. It looks as though the roof's about to fall in.'

We walked over to the shed together and I had a look at the sagging roofline. 'Nothing too serious, Mary,' I said. 'The basic structure is still sound; it just needs a few extra struts put in. I don't think there were enough there when the job was done. But it'll have to be done pretty quickly otherwise everything's going to start sagging, and you'll lose your iron.'

'It won't cost too much, will it, Charger?' Mary asked worriedly. 'It's just that I'm a little short till after the shearing, and I don't know if I can — '

'It won't cost you a thing, Mary,' I cut in. 'I've got some timber left over at Jim Clayton's place from that woolshed job I did for him. I'll pick it up and have that roof of yours fixed by the end of the week. And don't worry about labour charges either,' I added with a grin. 'You can show me some of those dog training secrets of yours and we'll call it even.'

Mary smiled, looking very relieved. 'Sounds like a good deal, Charger.'

I called in to see Jim Clayton a couple of days later. I wanted to discuss some club business with him and thought I'd pick up the timber for Mary's car shed while I was there. Jim was just putting his dogs away and had a couple of nice looking three-quarter-grown porkers hanging in the woolshed.

'Nice looking pair, Jim. Where'd you score those?'

'Just behind the boundary fence,' Jim indicated with a nod of his head, 'out towards Mason's Gully, not far from where Miles got ripped up. His own bloody fault too, mucking around like that.'

Never having heard Jim's account of the accident, I was suddenly very interested. 'What d'you mean mucking about?' I asked.

Jim rubbed his chin thoughtfully. 'Well, maybe I shouldn't speak ill of the dead and maybe he wasn't really mucking about, but he should have climbed above that boar instead of taking the easy way out and approaching it from below the way he did. He couldn't see where he was going anyway, with all that scrub between him and the boar. Mary was up above yelling directions down to him, telling him which way to go, but I don't think he could hear her properly what with all the noise going on from the dogs. He kept going the wrong way. He got it right in the end though. I could see he was directly below the boar in a straight line with only about twenty yards separating the two. I remember thinking at the time that if the boar broke loose he'd be in trouble, but the dogs seemed to be holding okay. Mary was getting quite excited and she yelled out to him, "That's it, Miles, keep going, you're onto it." Then she started clapping her hands. I suppose she was just applauding his efforts — '

'Yes, Jim,' I interrupted, 'I suppose that's what anybody would think.'

CHAPTER 5

Professional Secrets

Claude Jackson had the smallest property in the valley, just the three acres, but he made a passable living off it selling eggs and vegetables to a couple of hotels in town and from his front gate to passers-by. Full credit to him too. Making a living off a place that small would have required some very shrewd management plus a lot of hard work and Claude was no spring chicken. According to everybody's reckoning he had to be somewhere in his mid seventies but he got around all right despite having something of a physical handicap with one leg being shorter than the other.

In an attempt to overcome the problem he always wore a boot with a built-up sole, about three inches thick. This helped a bit but he still walked with a noticeable limp that was more pronounced during bouts of cold weather. Usually old people living on their own appreciate a bit of company but Claude was the exception. He made every visitor feel about as welcome as a Jehovah's Witness selling Amway products.

In the end none of us locals bothered to make any social calls. In fact the only reason I called round that particular day was to use his phone. I'd been giving the dogs a run over the long-since abandoned

Rumai Station which more or less overlooked Claude's place when I came across a deserted camp site. There was a sheet of canvas slung over a rope suspended between a couple of tawas acting as a tent and inside it I found a pack, a couple of army blankets and a lever action Marlin rifle. It was a bit hard to tell but it looked as though whoever had set the camp up hadn't been near the place for a couple of days so I figured the missing party was either lost or injured. I didn't waste any time getting to Claude's place and caught the old bloke in his long underpants and socks sitting in front of his kitchen fire reading the Sunday papers. 'I need to use your phone, Claude, if that's okay,' I said, putting the pack and rifle down in a spare corner. Claude glanced over then nodded towards the phone which I assumed was his way of saying it was all right for me to use it.

I got through to the police station without any trouble but the officious sounding constable on the other end was a real pain. He was writing down everything I said word for word and wanted to know where the campsite was, what kind of pack and rifle I'd found, had I noticed any suspicious circumstances, was I acquainted with the missing party and did I have any 'topographical knowledge' of the area.

I told him it would be a good idea to send someone over because it would be a whole lot quicker for me to show them than for me to tell him. He got real snotty with me over that and told me in no uncertain terms that the New Zealand police force had been managing quite well without my help for years and felt certain they could manage any foreseeable emergencies in the future but he agreed to send somebody over anyway. I hung the phone up and Claude surprised me by actually getting up and putting the kettle on for a brew. He even got two mugs down from the shelf and invited me to sit down while he fussed around putting condensed milk and sugar in the mugs. He kept glancing over at the rifle too. I could see he was working himself up to say something. 'They shouldn't have any trouble tracing the owner of that Marlin,' he said. 'It's a model 93 sporting carbine in 30-30; you don't see too many of them around. The Marlin company started turning them out in 1923. They got so popular the company was having trouble keeping up with demand so not too many of them found their way over here and that's a pity. It's only my opinion but I reckon it was one of the best lever action sporting rifles ever made. It's got a five-round mag and that's plenty if you can shoot, ballard-type rifling for accuracy, rocky mountain sights for fast aiming and it only weighs about six and a half pounds. Pretty good package whichever way you look at it,' Claude concluded, reaching for the teapot.

I was too flabbergasted to say anything. The old bloke had just spoken more words to me in the last ten minutes than he had in the preceding ten years and on top of that he'd spoken knowledgeably on a subject that nobody had any knowledge he was so knowledgeable about. Claude had never been known as a hunter or a shooter and there he was spouting off about Marlin rifles like he'd founded the company. I was going to ask him about it but Claude was inclined to get hostile if you got too inquisitive.

The police along with a dozen or so search and rescue volunteers showed up an hour and a half later and after I took them up to the campsite they organised a search. They found the missing hunter lying at the bottom of a gully just five minutes away from his camp. He'd wandered off looking for a creek to fill the billy and had taken a fall, breaking his leg and dislocating his shoulder in the process.

The S & R team got him out of there in record time and later on that evening one of them rang from the hospital to say his condition was satisfactory and to thank me for my help. A nice gesture, especially as they were the ones who had done all the work.

A week later it was all forgotten about and we were all getting on with our lives in the valley. Lambing was only a few weeks away and a few of the cockies were already starting to worry. The year before had been the worst season for lamb killers anyone could remember. The pigs had been real cheeky: on some properties, the more isolated ones, they'd been seen scoffing into the lambs right in the middle of the day.

George Sutton had lost so many he'd been on the verge of bankruptcy and his neighbours, Phil Roberts and Bob Cochrane, hadn't fared much better. It was so bad that stock and property owners were posting bounties: anything up to five quid for any known lamb killer, with sows and half-grown pigs fetching anything from ten bob to a quid a time. That was pretty good money back in the early 1950s. Sammy Mita and I had been in the last year of our apprenticeships, getting paid almost as much as indentured tradesmen, yet we made more money on weekends that year during the lambing season pighunting than we did at our regular jobs. So while all the cockies were hoping the pigs would stay away that year we were hoping they wouldn't. Of course we didn't tell anybody that; there was no point in going out of our way to be unpopular.

Within a week of the first lambs being born in the valley all the signs were pointing to another bad year for lamb killers. Sammy couldn't wait to get round and tell me that George Sutton and Phil Roberts had already been hit. He was trying not to look happy about it, but you could see he was. 'George and Phil are offering a flat rate of a quid for every pig we get but they don't want us using dogs,' Sammy explained. 'They reckon the dogs will upset their ewes too much.'

Not being able to use the dogs wasn't too much of a problem as Sammy and I had done okay in the past sneaking along the bush in the early mornings and bowling the pigs over that way, but I was in need of a new rifle. My old .303 which I'd had for about four years had been used for everything from a billy hook to a tyre lever when I wasn't actually shooting it, and not surprisingly wasn't shooting the best any more. The barrel was nickled up too, making it kick like a mule and incapable of any degree of accuracy. I could have borrowed one without any trouble but it's not something I like doing, and going into town to get a new one, going through all the permit to procure rigmarole at the police station, was impossible for the next couple of weeks at least. My boss had me building a new implement shed at Johnny McDowell's place in the Ahu Ahu Valley and we were flat out with more work coming in all the time. Taking a half day off to go into town just to buy a rifle wouldn't have gone down too well at all.

I was still trying to figure a way round the problem when a parcel with my name on it got dropped off at the gate. My mother brought it in, holding it as though it were about to explode. She was always nervous of parcels, was Mum, it was almost a phobia with her. I didn't have a clue what was in it and got quite a surprise to find myself looking at the Marlin I'd found seven weeks before. There was a letter with it from the injured hunter. I can't remember his last name and I'm having difficulty trying to recall his first, but I think it was Stuart and he was definitely from Palmerston North.

In his letter he said that his hunting trip into the valley had been his first and last. According to Stuart he simply wasn't cut out for it. He was also of the opinion that if I hadn't found his camp and raised the alarm his injuries could well have proved fatal as he would never have got out of that gully without assistance. As a token of his appreciation he was giving me the Marlin, insisting he had no further use for it. At first I didn't feel too comfortable about keeping it. I'd really only done what anyone else would have done in the same circumstances but at the same time it seemed pointless to send it back if it wasn't going to be used.

In the end I decided to hang on to it for a couple of days and after that I got quite accustomed to the idea of keeping it. Compared to the old .303 that Marlin was a flash piece of work, and taking proper care of it was something I needed to learn.

My old man wasn't much help; neither was Ted Thompson, even though he'd been hunting all his life. 'Can't help you there, mate,' he said. 'Never had much to do with them cowboy guns.'

Calling in on old Claude was the obvious thing to do, but with him being such a grumpy old sod it took me a couple of days to get round to it. When I did call round the old bloke actually looked pleased to see me or maybe he just wanted to have another look at the Marlin. As soon as I told him why I was there he took me into his workshop, rummaged around for a cleaning rod and some cloth patches and showed me what to do. It seemed a long and complicated process at the time but it wasn't really, just a case of me being unfamiliar with it. The only maintenance my old .303 ever got was to get the water shaken out of it after a fall in the creek.

By the time we'd finished there was just enough daylight left to fire off a few shots. Claude drew a cross on a cardboard box for me and showed me how to load the Marlin, not forgetting to tell me that I was never to walk around with 'one up the spout' because that practice was even more dangerous when using any kind of firearm with an exposed hammer. The Marlin handled like a dream, was bang on accurate and as the light began to fade I discovered the value of having an ivory bead foresight. It stuck out like the proverbial sore thumb, giving a really clear sight picture — not as good as a scope of course, but heaps better than ordinary iron sights.

When it got too dark to do anything else Claude took me back into his workshop and stood over me while I cleaned the Marlin all over again. Just as I was finishing, his phone rang and while he was inside the house answering it I had a nosey round his workshop. There wasn't much to see but under his bench I found piles of Western paperbacks. There must have been over a hundred of them, mostly by authors such as Zane Grey and O. Henry but there were a few others as well. There was also a big coloured advertising poster for Buffalo Bill's Wild West Show pinned up on the wall, dated 1901. It had a picture of the man himself sitting on a horse, proclaiming him as the world's greatest buffalo hunter, Indian fighter and scout, and there was a smaller picture of Annie Oakley announcing her as the world's greatest markswoman. It was real authentic looking and I guessed it to be an original. There was a lot of other stuff written on it too but Claude came back before I could read it all. It didn't really matter; I wasn't all that interested but finding out that old Claude was something of a Wild West fan gave some kind of an explanation for him knowing so much about Marlin rifles.

After thanking Claude for his trouble I left, promising to call in again with a nice eating-size porker as soon as I got one. Claude just shrugged as though he couldn't have cared less, but then he had an afterthought. 'I don't go much on wild pork,' he said, 'but I wouldn't say no to a bit of venison if you get any.'

On Friday night Sammy called round to see if I was still on for the weekend. I told him I was and he talked enthusiastically about all the pigs we were going to get. 'We'll make a pile of dough this season, Charger, you'll see,' he said. 'We might even make enough to shout ourselves a holiday overseas or maybe a flash car each, eh?'

'I'll be happy with just a new pair of boots, Sammy,' I said. 'The ones I'm wearing have worn down so much I can stand on a coin and tell you whether it's heads or tails.' Sammy didn't get the joke but he had a vague idea I'd made one so he laughed just to be polite. Sammy was like that, real easy to get along with, though when I called round to pick him up at 4.30 next morning he wasn't looking quite so enthusiastic — more like death warmed up. All the way out to

George Sutton's place Sammy sat shivering, sniffing and wiping his nose on the sleeve of his bush shirt. Not much for conversation.

An hour and a half later we were sneaking through the bush overlooking George Sutton's lamb paddocks when Sammy started pointing excitedly off to the right somewhere. He'd spotted a mob of about a dozen pigs of various sizes mooching around in the paddock and he was already counting the money. We knew the pigs would head straight for the bush as soon as we started firing so we moved down to cut off their retreat. Everything was going okay but then Sammy slipped over on something, which was enough to spook the mob. We managed to drop four before they got under cover, or rather I did, because Sammy hadn't fired a shot. 'Couldn't get this bloody gun of mine to work, eh,' he said disgustedly, 'just like that bloody brother-in-law of mine.'

I had a look at Sammy's .303 — it was in an even worse state than my old one. 'The bolt's rusted up, Sammy,' I told him. 'I can't even get it open. When was the last time you cleaned this thing?'

Sammy thought about it for a couple of seconds. 'Hasn't been that long. I gave it a good clean after we got back from that trip in the Ruahines.'

'Bloody hell, Sammy, that was two years ago.'

'Yeah?'

'Yeah!'

We moved another hour along the bush edge and I nailed another two boars on Phil Roberts' place. One of them was still feeding on a newborn lamb. All told Sammy and me had made half a week's wages each for a morning's work.

The next day we hit George's place again but only managed a couple of slab-sided sows. Despite all the early signs the pigs didn't prove too much of a problem that year but Sammy and I didn't do too badly. I was able to shout myself a new pair of boots and bush shirt and get a new set of tyres for the Ford. The old ones were down to the canvas. Determined to have his holiday, Sammy took off to stay with relatives in sunny Hawke's Bay. It rained every day for the two weeks he was there.

Things were starting to change on the pighunting scene. Whereas before few pighunters had owned rifles and even fewer had ever bothered carrying them, firearms were beginning to play a more prominent role in the sport. The boars were getting faster and meaner and showing more cunning, and hard-bailing dogs that were usually faster and quicker on their feet than holders were becoming fashionable. Bailers would still go in and hold sows or small pigs but would show enough sense to stand back on anything carrying ivory, leaving you to finish things with a well-placed shot behind the ear or shoulder. Maybe it wasn't quite so adventurous but a man wasn't making nearly as many trips to the vet either. Some blokes used .303's with shortened barrels which did the job okay but I felt a whole lot better off with the Marlin. It was short, lightweight, hard hitting, accurate and fast handling, a pretty good package, just like old Claude said it was.

We had a good summer that year; not too hot and with just enough rain to keep the cockies happy. The river was fishing well, the hunting was good and I remembered to get a fallow deer for Claude just in time for Christmas. There's quite a bit of meat on a full-grown fallow buck, too much for a bloke living on his own, but that didn't worry Claude. 'I'll make jerky out of it,' he said. 'It'll keep for months.' I had no idea what jerky was back then but I told Claude it sounded like a good idea then sat back and watched him go to work.

After skinning the deer in about five minutes flat Claude boned out all the meat which he then cut into long thin strips. Each strip then had to be given a gentle sprinkling of salt on both sides and left for about an hour while Claude rigged up the drying rack. It was a simple thing: just four posts stuck in the ground with some chicken wire stretched over the top like a hammock. After laying all the strips of meat on the wire he then got a manuka fire going underneath. The idea was to have plenty of smoke but very little heat. This way the meat would dry right out before being cooked and that's what enhanced its keeping qualities. I helped as much as I could though Claude seemed to have everything under control.

This drying process would take anything up to eight hours so, not being able to stick around that long, I headed into town to catch up on some Christmas shopping. Everybody else in the district must have had the same idea. Parking places were as rare as honest politicians and to add to the excitement the circus had come to town. There were clowns running up and down the main street handing out pamphlets to the grown-ups and lollies to the kids. I must have posed some kind of a problem for them because I got one of each. I gave the lolly to a kid and told him it was Christmas. He said he already knew that so I took the lolly back and gave him the pamphlet. I'd finished reading it anyway. It advertised all the things you expect to see at a circus like clowns and acrobats and trapeze artists but this one had the added attraction of a cowboy sharpshooter.

I called in to Claude's place on the way home to tell him about it, thinking he'd be interested, but he wasn't, though he did thank me again for the venison and gave me a box full of eggs and vegetables to take home for Mum.

Sammy and I, along with practically everybody else in the valley, went along on Boxing Day when the circus opened and it was quite a good show. I can't speak for everybody but Sammy and I were looking forward to seeing the cowboy sharpshooter more than anything else and we had to wait right till the end because his act was the grand finale. Before he could perform his act a safety wall of sandbags had to be put up and while this was being done a juggler came out to keep us entertained but we weren't. His entire act consisted of juggling three oranges and taking a bow every time he dropped one. Finally it was time for the sharpshooter.

He was introduced as Luke Lane, the world's greatest sharpshooter, all the way from San Antonio, Texas. He came riding in on a big white horse, dressed up in Western gear and wearing a big white hat. There was a girl with him too, also riding a horse and wearing a big white hat but the rest of her outfit was a bit on the skimpy side, only just managing to cover the bits that mattered. Apart from giving some of the young blokes and all of the old blokes a bit of a thrill prancing around like that it was hard to see where she fitted in.

The first thing that Luke did was shoot the centre out of the ace of spades which, at a distance of only fifteen metres, was only mildly impressive, but then he moved on to slightly better things. The next part of Luke's act consisted of him shooting at some metal duck silhouettes that were moving along on a conveyor belt type thing. He hit 10 out of 10 and got some applause but I didn't think it was enough to earn him the title of the world's greatest. There were at least half a dozen blokes from the valley I knew who could have matched it or at least come close.

Luke's next trick was to shoot a cigar in half that the ringmaster was holding in his mouth. This brought on another round of applause but I still wasn't overly impressed. It was a big cigar. I was starting to think the whole thing was a bit of a rip-off when Luke went into his final act and that was impressive. A couple of the circus blokes brought out a tripod with a wagon wheel mounted on it. Around the rim of the wheel were six coloured balloons but they were only small, about the size of a tennis ball. As soon as everything was set up Luke opened up a flash-looking gun case and pulled out a very flash-looking Winchester rifle. He then spoke into the microphone telling us all that it was a Winchester 73, the gun that won the West. He also claimed that the one he was holding had once belonged to Buffalo Bill himself, but I think a few of us had our doubts about that.

Luke then got himself ready, standing about twenty metres away from the wagon wheel, and at this moment the ringmaster called for silence. You could feel the tension. Then the ringmaster stepped forward and gave the spin. It was going at a fair rate of knots when Luke started firing and he hit all six balloons with all six shots and this time I applauded with everybody else. It was good shooting all right, about the best I'd ever seen. Just to show it wasn't a fluke the ringmaster announced that Luke would perform the trick again and he did, hitting six out of six in rapid succession. There was lots of cheering and clapping and we all felt we'd had our money's worth. As soon as we stepped outside I headed for the pie cart and Sammy said he'd see me later. He was off to get Luke's autograph.

I was halfway through my second pie when Sammy caught up with me looking real pleased with himself. He'd not only got Luke Lane's autograph but had managed to talk him into putting on a show for us at our rod and gun club gala that we held every year to raise funds for the Crippled Children's Association. 'He's not even going to charge us either,' Sammy ended. 'Pretty good, eh?'

'Yeah, Sammy, pretty good.'

The gala was scheduled for the following Saturday and we had everything ready before the crowd started arriving. We had coconut stands, lolly scrambles and lucky dips for the kids, a wheel of fortune, a big table with numbers on it where you rolled a penny down a slotted ramp and tried to land it on a winning number to get a prize, and lots of other things too. Luke turned up in one of the circus vans with the girl who had been part of his act. She didn't look anywhere near as good up close wearing ordinary clothes and Sammy was heartbroken. 'Bloody hell, even my sister is better looking than her,' he moaned.

Luke got his wagon wheel set up and put into place then went into the club rooms to change into his cowboy outfit. The crowds were just starting to build up and Luke got all of us committee members together. He had a proposition to put to us, what he called 'An offer we couldn't refuse.' He said he was quite happy to put on a show and provided we accepted his conditions he would even go so far as to make a generous donation to the charity.

'Just what are the conditions and how generous is the donation?' Ted Thompson asked, and Luke explained it all. He would put on a show for free just like he said he would and he would offer a prize of fifty pounds to anyone who could hit three of the six balloons on the spinning wagon wheel out of six shots in under a minute. The contest would be open to all comers and they could use their own rifles if they wished or use either of the two spare Winchesters he'd brought along which we were free to inspect and test fire for accuracy. He added this bit because he wanted everything to be above board and beyond reproach. If anyone did manage to hit three out of six of the balloons then not only would he hand over the fifty pound prize but he would also donate a further fifty pounds to the club's charity. Each contestant would have to pay a fee of 2/6 which would go into the hat and this too in the event of somebody winning would go to the Crippled Children's Association.

'What happens if nobody hits three out of six?' Phil Collins, our club treasurer, asked.

'Then I hang on to my one hundred pounds and take whatever's in the hat,' Luke answered matter of factly. 'It's only fair, I'm the one who's prepared to risk one hundred pounds and put on a show for free. You guys think it over and let me know what you decide.'

We huddled together for a quick conference and decided that

Luke's proposition was fair enough. We were being given the opportunity to make some money for a worthy cause and the only person who could actually lose on the deal was Luke himself, so we said okay. Ted Thompson got on the loudspeaker and announced our special attraction to a crowd that had swelled to almost twice as many as we had the year before. Sammy and his dad, Awhi, test fired the spare Winchesters and declared them 'kapai'.

Luke put on a couple of shows shooting the balloons on the turning wagon wheel, making it look easy, then the challenge was issued to all comers willing to risk 2/6 to have a go. There was no shortage of takers but hitting those balloons was a hell of a lot harder than it looked. Most of the blokes who had a go failed to hit any and even some of the best shots in the valley could only manage to hit one. The only person to hit two was Spencer Barton but it cost him half a quid because he had four goes at it.

I was tempted to go home and get the Marlin and have a go but chickened out on the grounds of not wanting to make a fool of myself like everybody else was doing. Luke's act was really drawing the crowds. The money in the hat was piling up and looked as though it was going to end up in his pocket. It was good to see so many people there even if it was getting too crowded to move around without bumping into people.

I stepped to one side to make room for a woman who was obviously pregnant and collided with another woman who was obviously fat. At the moment of impact she was taking a bite of hot dog and it ended up halfway down her throat. Before I had a chance to apologise for something that was only an accident anyway she let rip with a mouthful of abuse, tomato sauce and bits of batter and saveloy. Her husband tried calming her down because he could see it hadn't been intentional and then she started on him. I lost myself in the crowd while they were arguing and then somebody stepped on my foot. It felt like a horse. I looked up; it was Claude and he'd stepped on me with that big boot of his. 'Sorry, young fella,' he said, 'I'm just having a bit of trouble getting around this crowd; and what's all the shooting about?'

'It's a contest,' I explained, 'a shooting contest put on by Luke Lane, the cowboy sharpshooter from the circus. Come on over and see for yourself.'

Claude and I pushed our way through the crowd and saw that Luke was still getting plenty of takers and that big white hat of his was three-quarters full of silver coins. Claude wanted to know what the rules were so I told him. 'You're sure I can use my own rifle?' he asked.

'One hundred percent sure,' I said.

'And what charity is it for?' he wanted to know.

'It's for the crippled children, Claude,' I said, and felt a bit embarrassed under the circumstances. Claude patted me on the shoulder. 'Don't feel bad, young fella,' he said. 'I was born with a big foot and a short leg and it's nobody's fault, just one of those things. But it isn't so bad. I was never able to play any sport and I wasn't very good in the one hundred yard dash but I got around, so do me a favour and see if you can hold a place in the queue for me. I'll be back in half an hour.'

I couldn't actually hold a place in the queue for Claude but I hung around till he got back anyway. He came back carrying something wrapped in japara cloth and I didn't need to be a rocket scientist to guess it was a rifle and a Marlin at that. Claude waited his turn then dropped 2/6 in the hat before unwrapping his rifle. 'I see you've brought your own hardware, old-timer,' Luke called out cheerfully. But Claude wasn't amused.

'It's not bloody hardware, it's a Marlin 44-40 and my name isn't old-timer,' he told Luke.

'No offence meant, sir,' Luke apologised. 'I'll give the wheel a spin whenever you're ready.'

'I'd like a bit of quiet first,' Claude said, stepping forward and loading his rifle. And everybody in the immediate vicinity stood silent. It was as if we were all getting behind the old bloke and I suppose we were, even if the most optimistic ones among us didn't think he had a chance in hell of pulling it off. Claude gave a nod to say he was ready and Luke gave the wheel a spin. Claude had 60 seconds in which to fire six shots and hit at least three of those coloured balloons to win the money.

Thirty seconds ticked by and Claude didn't make a move. I guessed that he was waiting for the wheel to slow down a bit. A few of the other jokers had tried that dodge but the wheel didn't slow down all that much and the longer Claude waited the less time he was going to have to get his shots off.

Forty seconds ticked by and I was starting to worry but then Claude put the Marlin to his shoulder and fired off three evenly spaced shots in about ten seconds, maybe even less than that; I forgot to count. We stood there with our mouths wide open not daring to believe it. Luke stood there with his mouth wide open not wanting to believe it but there was no denying Claude had pulled it off. He'd hit three balloons with three shots and had made it look as though it was an everyday thing for him.

'How much does he get if he hits the other three?' somebody in the crowd yelled out, but Luke Lane wasn't having that on. He handed the money in the hat over to Ted plus the fifty pounds promised, gave Claude his fifty pounds then had his girlfriend pack the gear up. He didn't look very happy. People were clapping and cheering and slapping Claude on the back but you could tell he didn't want a fuss made. He shrugged it all off then went over to Ted and gave him the fifty pounds he'd just won.

'That's for the crippled kids,' he said, then walked off before anyone could thank him.

Not surprisingly this episode became the most talked-about event in the valley since our mobile librarian, Miss Fay Courtney, had got pregnant to our very upstanding minister, the Reverend Duncan Seymour. More than anything I wanted to call in on Claude and see if I could find out anything. Like where the hell did he learn to shoot like that? But I decided against it and hoped that maybe I'd catch him in a talkative mood one day.

Almost a month went by before I did visit Claude again. He was walking up and down between his rows of cabbages carrying a .22 rifle which of course was a Marlin too. 'The bloody rabbits are getting more of my carrots than I am,' he grumbled, and just as he spoke one of them took off across his onion patch. It was only about twenty metres away and not moving all that fast but Claude didn't even come close to hitting it with three shots so I didn't think it was an appropriate time to talk about his sharpshooting. We talked about the weather instead and before I left he gave me some more eggs and vegetables to take home and some of his venison jerky. It was good too, real tasty in fact, though perhaps a little on the salty side for some people.

By the time Easter rolled round that year Claude's shooting performance at the gala had been relegated to ancient history by almost everybody, but hardly a day went by without me thinking about it. Claude's performance would have been considered exceptional if he'd been a young man who practised on a daily basis but for an old man who'd never been known to practise at all and who had missed a rabbit at twenty metres it was beyond credibility. I needed something to take my mind off it — it was becoming an obsession — so when Sammy invited me to visit his relatives in Hawke's Bay for a few days I was happy to accept.

'The pighunting is pretty good in the Mohaka, Charger,' he said, and I believed him. 'I hear they get 500-pound boars from there all the time,' he added, and I didn't believe him, but figured we'd have some fun finding out anyway.

Sammy's relatives were easygoing and friendly and if you went hungry at their place it was your own fault. When they said 'Make yourself at home,' or 'Help yourself,' that's exactly what they meant. There was Uncle Huia and Aunty Coral, their three sons Antony, Ricky and Benjamin, plus their two daughters Moana and Aroha, and Coral's younger sister Tania who was about the same age as me. She lived in Auckland but was down having a few days' holiday as well. Their home was situated on Maori land not too far from the Mohaka River and Uncle Huia proudly told everybody it was the best place in the world. 'We grow our own vegetables and meat only costs the price of a bullet,' he said on an average of six times a day.

Tania took a shine to me right from the start which was handy because I'd already taken a shine to her. I would have been quite happy to give the pighunting a miss but Sammy was champing at the bit to get going so love had to be put on hold for a while. The fern- and scrub-covered slopes that led down to the river certainly held high numbers of pigs, though 500-pounders were a bit scarce. In under four hours we scored a 150-pound one-eyed boar and four half-grown pigs that Sammy's Auntie Coral was going to make pickled pork out of. We thought we had enough but then the dogs took off again and grabbed a huge barrow that weighed just under 200 pounds.

Getting more meat than we could carry seemed to be a problem, especially for Uncle Huia. He took a dim view of leaving meat on the hill. Then Sammy hit on the idea of going back to the house for the pack horse. There was no point in us both going so as Sammy headed off I dropped down to the river to try out a bit of fishing. I had a few metres of line and some hooks in the pikau and a length of manuka made up my outfit. Finding some crickets for bait didn't take very long either. I was keen to catch one of these fantastic Mohaka rainbows that everybody told me never came under ten pounds in weight.

I spent over an hour trying the likeliest looking pools without any luck when a voice called out for me to fish the shallows above the head of the main pool. It was Tania. She'd brought the pack horse because Sammy was too stuffed to make the return journey. 'Try the shallows,' she repeated. 'There's always trout there in the middle of the day. They love to feel the sun on their backs.'

I couldn't see any trout sunning themselves but gave it a try anyway with a fresh cricket. I cast upstream and watched the line swing round when a thumping great rainbow darted out from behind a rock and swallowed the cricket like it hadn't had a feed for a month. That rainbow was twice as big as anything I'd caught before and I started to buckle under the pressure. It wouldn't have mattered if I'd been alone but with Tania there squealing and giggling and clapping her hands I was scared to death of losing it. The trout shot off downstream and I had no choice but to splash on through the rapids after it.

Tania thought it was a hell of a joke and joined in. She'd get below the trout and scare it upstream then get above it and chase it back down, the idea being to tire it out. We were getting soaked to the skin, laughing and carrying on like a couple of kids. After what seemed for ever I managed to coax the trout onto a shingle bar with only a couple of inches covering it and the hook came out. Tania and I dived on the fish like a pair of All Black forwards on a loose ball. One of us would get hold of it and it would wriggle free then the other one would make a grab for it and have the same thing happen.

Finally I managed to hold onto it for long enough to heave it high onto the bank. We were laughing so much we could scarcely get our breath then we were hugging and kissing each other just like a scene from a movie. Breaking the ice like that was a godsend for me because I wasn't very good at chatting up girls; bloody hopeless in fact. But it didn't seem to matter with Tania. I didn't feel the need to be witty or charming; we were happy just to share each other's company and talk about anything that came to mind.

After tea that night we sat on the back porch and watched the sun go down. Courting couples did a lot of that before the days of television. We sat there making occasional remarks about what a beautiful night it was then Tania asked me about my Marlin. I told her the full story of how I'd come to get it, adding a few extra bits just to make it sound more interesting and make me look a bit more of a hero, and she seemed impressed. Then she asked me what I thought of the 30-30, how I rated its performance compared to the .303 or any others I might have used. Just by the way she was talking you could tell she had a few clues on the subject and that's when she told me she worked for the Colonial Ammunition Company in Auckland.

It was my turn to be impressed. I listened with interest as she told me all about her job. Making ammunition was much more of a science than I'd ever thought it was and everything had to be exactly right. As we were on the subject anyway I told her all about Claude's fancy bit of shooting. 'There has to be some logical explanation for it,' I said and she laughed out loud.

'Of course there is,' she said, 'but I don't know if I should tell you.'

'Tell me anyway,' I insisted.

Tania looked around as if to make sure nobody else was listening. 'Well it's like this,' she explained. 'The wagon wheel always has the same number of spokes as it does targets. They might be glass balls or clay pipes or, as they were in this case, balloons, it doesn't really matter. What is important is that you have the same number of spokes as you do targets and you have those targets positioned on the rim of the wheel exactly halfway between the spokes. This is because behind each spoke there's a strip of leather which strikes against the tripod and makes a dull slapping sound. That tells the shooter when to fire. All he has to do is line up on the top of the wheel and squeeze the trigger when he hears that slap. That's why the shooter always asks for silence. He can't afford to miss hearing that sound. If he does he's likely to miss.'

'You'd still have to be a bloody good shot, though,' I said, and Tania laughed again.

'Not really,' she said, 'because they use special rifles and ammunition. The rifles are smooth bored like a shotgun and the ammunition is made like a shotgun cartridge loaded with fine birdshot instead of a solid lead bullet.'

As incredible as it all sounded I could see that Tania's explanation, if not the only one possible, had to be the most probable. 'How did you find out about all this?' I asked, still trying to sort everything out in my head.

Tania took another look around before answering. 'Well as I said in the beginning, I don't know if I should have told you because I don't want to get anyone into trouble. But about a month ago we had a visit from an American sales rep from one of the big companies over there. He was here on holiday and had been doing some research on trick shooting and found out some of the professional secrets used by sharpshooting performers. He intends to write a book about it. That's why he asked me not to say anything because some of the methods he used to get his information hadn't been strictly within the law.'

'So none of this is public knowledge then, Tania?' I asked, just to make sure I'd got my facts straight.

'Good heavens no,' Tania replied. 'Just think of all the outcry if it became public knowledge, and it would put a lot of sharpshooting acts out of business. It's a big thing over in the States and still draws the crowds in England and Europe so I'm told.'

By telling me what she had Tania had solved one mystery but at the same time given me another one to work on. If all these professional secrets had been kept under wraps for so long, how had Claude found out about them and how was I going to find out how he found out? I couldn't just walk up to him and ask him outright because Tania had made me promise not to say anything. It seemed as though Claude's secret was one he'd take to the grave and he might have done too if fate hadn't stepped in.

It was all of twelve months later. Tania had moved in with Sammy's family, had got a job in town and we were still seeing each other though on what you might call a platonic level. Her birthday was coming up on Easter Monday so Sammy and I had taken the dogs out for a run to scare up a bit of pork for the hangi that his old man had planned for the occasion. He always put down a good hangi, did Sammy's dad. Everything cooked to a turn, moist and full of flavour.

The hunting was hard that day, partly I think because some deerstalkers out for the roar had been thrashing our favourite bit of bush but mostly because we were breaking in a couple of new dogs and the hunting's always harder when you're doing that. We did all right in the end though; we just had to up our workload a bit. We got three nice eating-size pigs and on the way back I dropped a fallow spiker with the Marlin just five minutes away from the truck. Sammy agreed we had more than enough meat for the hangi so that evening I drove round to Claude's place to drop off the spiker. I hadn't seen him in a while and was looking forward to a good yarn even if I was invariably the one who had to do all the talking.

I'd just coaxed the old Ford over the last hill before his place when I saw the flames and buried the boot. Claude had been burning some rubbish and it had got out of control on him. The flames were threatening his workshop and he was beating at them frantically with a wet sack and not doing much good with it. I jumped out of the Ford and screamed at him to get the hose then raced inside the workshop to clear everything away from the north wall, the one closest to the flames. He had a lot of flammable stuff in there and I knew if that caught alight then the whole place would go up with a bang. As it was, the smoke was already working its way through the weatherboards. My eyes were watering and I was coughing hard enough to bring on a hernia but I managed to shift everything back then raced outside to give Claude a hand.

With him on the hose and me with the wet sack we finally put the fire out but it took some doing. Claude was just about out on his feet so I talked him into going inside and making a cup of tea. 'I'll take care of things here, mate,' I promised.

While Claude was in the house making a brew I opened the windows of his workshop to let the smoke out then had a look around for any damage. There didn't seem to be any but I did notice a few smoke stains on Claude's Wild West poster, the one with Buffalo Bill and Annie Oakley on it. I knew he took pride in that poster so I grabbed a wet cloth and gently rubbed away at the stains. And that's when I saw it.

Underneath the big headlines that told you all about Buffalo Bill and Annie Oakley there was some smaller printing and it read: See and be amazed by the outstanding feats of marksmanship from our own Texas Jack Carver and Arizona's Billy Grant and our special feature all the way from the Antipodes in the far away South Pacific, New Zealand's own Claude 'Big Foot' Jackson.

I must have read that line a dozen times before Claude yelled out to tell me he'd poured the tea. Sitting there at the table with the old bloke, knowing what I knew but not being able to say anything, was one of the most difficult situations I'd ever handled.

'You're quiet tonight, young fella,' he said. 'Something on your mind?'

Stalling for time I reached for my tobacco tin and began rolling a smoke. I had to choose my words carefully if I was to retain the old bloke's friendship which I valued highly. 'You've forgotten the sugar, mate,' I said.

CHAPTER 6

One and the Same

When Terry and Fran Lester celebrated the birth of their identical twin boys Chris and Wayne they had good cause to celebrate. Not only were Chris and Wayne the first set of identical twin boys to be born in the valley for as long as anyone could remember but after ten years of trying Terry and Fran had all but given up hope of ever becoming parents. It was quite a party by all accounts but I was only three days old at the time so I can't remember a hell of a lot about it.

What I do remember is growing up with Chris and Wayne and having as much difficulty in telling them apart as everybody else. They were a right pair of tearaways too, always getting themselves into scrapes and playing those tricks that identical twins play on people like swapping classrooms or girlfriends and pretending to be each other.

One of their favourite stunts was when they went to the movies. Chris would buy a ticket, walk up, show it to the usher then go inside and take a seat. Five minutes later he'd go back outside telling the usher to remember his face and that he was just going to the little boys' room. 'No problem, I'll remember,' the usher would say. A few minutes would go by then Wayne would walk up to the usher who would let him in thinking it was Chris. Then a few minutes after that Chris would go sauntering innocently up to the door and get challenged by the usher. 'Hey, hang on a minute, young fella,' the usher would say. 'I just let you in two minutes ago.'

'You couldn't have done,' Chris would argue, 'I've been in the toilet.'

'Well let's see your ticket, then,' the usher would demand, and Chris would show his ticket, leaving the usher with no choice but to let him in and spend the rest of the night wondering what the hell he'd struck. As they grew older their physical similarities seemed to grow stronger and they became harder than ever to tell apart. Even Terry and Fran had problems until Wayne developed a small mole on his chin and broke his ankle while we were giving the dogs a run at the back of John Maisey's place. We'd missed out on getting the pig too which didn't go down too well.

We got him to the hospital okay and he was on crutches for a while but for some reason or other his ankle didn't heal properly. He always walked with his foot turned in slightly after that, kind of pigeon-toed you might say, and it was more noticeable when he was running. Apart from this though, Chris and Wayne were still like two peas from the same pod and strangers could never tell one from the other.

Besides pighunting Chris and Wayne's other major interest and reason for living was amateur dramatics. You'd wonder how something like that could have held such an attraction for a pair of hardcases like those two, but it did. In fact, Wayne once admitted to me that if he had the choice between playing the lead role in *Oklahoma* or getting the best pair of tusks to ever come out of the valley, he'd give the ivory a miss without too much regret. Not that it made much difference at the end of the day. Whether on stage or in the hills the twins always gave plenty of value. They were always up in the top five whenever we had a biggest boar competition and you wouldn't get too much argument if you said that between the two of them they would have taken more wild pork out of the valley than any two hunters born.

They had a system I'd never seen used before and which as far as I know hasn't been used since, at least not as successfully. They only had the two dogs, a pair of huntaway lab crosses which you could put in the finder/bailer category and which were well suited to this particular method of hunting pigs. The two brothers would choose a likely looking gully, take a side each and begin walking slowly up towards the head. Two things were absolutely necessary for this system to work: the first being a tail wind, the stronger the better; and the second, they each had to know exactly where the other was at all times. That was the hard part.

When two blokes split up in the bush it's usually impossible for them to keep track of one another but Chris and Wayne never had a problem with this. It was as if they had built-in radar or a sixth sense. Even in those days I'd heard stories about how twins could tune in on each other using ESP or mental telepathy or something like that but this was one of the few times I'd actually seen it put into practice.

As the boys walked up towards the head of the gully the pigs, getting wind of their approach, would also start heading upwards, as if Chris and Wayne were herding them like a couple of shepherds. The boys had to keep spot-on parallel to each other, otherwise there'd be what they called 'a break in their scent'. Even though they might not be able to see each other, that ESP of theirs helped them to communicate in a way none of the rest of us could.

Once they had the pigs bunched up in the head of the gully they would either start shooting if they had a clear view of things or send in the dogs if they didn't. And those dogs of theirs deserve a mention. Like their masters they seemed to have some indefinable means of communication with each other as well. They would only go in on the pigs together, even if it meant one of them had to hang on and wait for the other to catch up, and if one of them was having trouble with a boar the other one would come in to lend a hand every time, even if it meant letting go of something he was holding.

The boys reckoned the dogs had worked this system out for themselves. They certainly hadn't had a hand in it. Sammy Mita and I tried working the gullies the same way as the twins with varying degrees of success, none of them worth mentioning, so I won't, but we did learn one thing to our advantage. Whenever we walked up a gully with the wind blowing from behind any pigs ahead of us would nearly always vacate the area using a single track. After sussing this out we worked out a system of one of us waiting in ambush on the track while the other walked up the gully. It worked often enough to prove a point if we'd been trying to prove one, which we weren't, and it was something of a novelty at first but the idea never caught on.

The results didn't really justify all the time and preparation needed for everything to go right so Sammy and I abandoned the idea along with a few others we'd had in the past. Though I think our plan for crossbreeding domestic fowls with emus would have been a moneyspinner if we'd ever got it started. 'Just think of it, Charger,' Sammy had said. 'One drumstick would feed a family.' Our main problem was getting our hands on some emus. We wrote to the Australian embassy about it but they must have thought we were having them on because they didn't even bother replying to our letter.

In addition to the one shilling per snout bounty the government was paying in those days a bloke could take his wild pork into town and sell it off to the game buyer for making into bacon but few of us ever bothered because of the low prices being offered. We either kept the pork for our own use or fed it to the dogs but that year pork prices soared. Supply couldn't keep up with demand and wild pork was fetching a shilling a pound. In practical terms this meant that a reasonable-sized pig was worth a week's wages so everybody bothered. We had hunters coming from as far away as Wellington to cash in on the boom. It was like a scene from a gold rush movie. Pig dogs became the most valuable commodity in the valley almost overnight, with mongrels barely worth their keep commanding unbelievable prices. Some of the locals got upset with what they regarded as an 'alien invasion' of their cherished hunting territory but most of us took it in our stride. We knew it wouldn't last and there'd be plenty of pigs left for us when it was over. And that's what happened.

Wild pork prices that had rocketed through the roof six months previously dive-bombed through the floor and things got back to normal or at least almost normal. We had witnessed a brief period of commercialism taking over recreational pighunting and hadn't been too impressed by it. Every pighunter worthy of the name knows it's a tough, physically demanding sport and expects to work hard for results, but that didn't stop some jokers from trying a few short cuts to make a quick and easy dollar. Trespassing, acts of vandalism, killing of stock and dog theft were frequent occurrences but the thing that really upset the locals was having their domesticated pigs stolen. Some of the low-lifes who couldn't get a pig the honest way were sneaking onto the farms after dark and making off with anything with trotters. By selling it off as wild pork the thieves didn't have to produce anything in the way of sales dockets or receipts and at first there didn't seem to be any way to combat the problem.

After getting their heads together the cockies came up with the scheme of insisting the buyers refuse payment on pigs that didn't have ears attached so they could be checked for tags. You didn't have to think about it for very long to see it was the obvious solution and everybody seemed happy with the idea, but then we weren't to know how much of a problem it was going to cause and how far reaching the effects would be.

We had a public notice put in the paper warning hunters of the new requirement and spread the news by word of mouth. Unfortunately neither Chris nor Wayne got to hear or read about it until it was too late. They'd been working their trap line for the last three months and came out with enough skins and wild pork loaded on pack horses to buy themselves the flash-looking V8 Chevrolet truck that was still sitting in Scotty Lloyd's used car yard. Scotty had promised the boys he'd hang on to it until they came out of the bush and give them first refusal. As far as Chris and Wayne were concerned that flash Chevy truck was as good as theirs.

It would have been too except for the changes that had taken place while they'd been away. The first bit of bad news the boys heard about was the drop in skin prices. They had over 500 first graders which would have paid for the truck outright had the market stayed buoyant but the most they could get was 2/6 each, the same as what the government bounty was worth at the time. It wasn't even enough for the deposit.

They were still feeling crushed by it all when they took their pork round to the meat buyer and that wasn't what you would call a happy occasion either. To save weight Chris and Wayne had cut the heads off their pigs just like we'd all been doing before the new ruling had gone into effect. It was a common enough practice because bringing pigs in with heads still attached was a waste of time and effort as buyers would deduct 10 percent off the weight before writing out a cheque. Dave Thompson, who happened to be Ted Thompson's nephew, had bought out the two partners who had previously owned the game meat buying business and it had fallen on him to break the news to Chris and Wayne. 'I'm sorry, boys,' he'd told them, 'but that's the way it is. I can't take any of your pork without heads or at least the ears.'

Neither of the boys liked what they were hearing but at least Wayne could see it wasn't anybody's fault, just the luck of the game. Chris wasn't quite so easily pacified though. He demanded to know who the hell had thought up the idea and even went so far as to accuse Dave of trying to rip them off. Dave tried explaining that by refusing their pork he was losing money as well, but Chris wouldn't listen. He heaped more abuse on Dave and it would have come to blows if I hadn't walked in right at that moment. While I wrestled with Dave to get him back behind the counter Wayne managed to shove his brother out the door. Word about the altercation went through the district like a plate of prunes and had the same unsettling effect.

As Ted Thompson's nephew, Dave was regarded as a local. He'd grown up in the valley and after a three-year spell in Auckland had come back, bought the game meat business as a sideline and was getting set to take over Ted's place as manager. This meant that Dave was going to stay local and the last thing we wanted was trouble among ourselves. Access to the valley had got easier over the years but we were still pretty much isolated. Because of this we had remained a close-knit community where we all relied on each other in times of need. Out of necessity, any differences of opinion or misunderstandings had to be settled quickly, without violence or any ill feeling at the end of it.

Wayne and Dave had put the episode behind them and were on friendly terms but Chris was still holding a grudge, we could all see that. He'd really had his heart set on that truck and blamed Dave for missing out on it. We all thought he'd get over it in time but it was going to take more than that. Even after twelve months when Dave moved onto Ted's place and threw a house-warming party that everyone in the district was invited to, Chris didn't bother to show. Wayne was there and seeing him without his brother made it all the more noticeable.

When Dave joined our rod and gun club, Chris immediately cancelled his membership. If Dave officiated at any of our pighunting competitions, then Chris wouldn't enter. If Dave walked into the Riverside Tavern while Chris was there then Chris would walk straight out the door. All this was having a negative effect on us so it must have been a worry for Dave, but his problems were only just starting.

He got up one morning to find a dozen of his in-lamb ewes lying in his road paddock with their throats cut. Just a few days after that somebody cut through his boundary fence and 30 of his steers had wandered off into the bush. It took him three days to find 22 of them and the rest were never seen again. Shortly after that somebody poisoned his water troughs and he ended up losing half the steers he'd brought back from the bush along with some sheep and two stock horses. Things had definitely got out of hand. We all had a good idea who was behind it all but knowing something is one thing, while proving it is often something else altogether.

The only thing we could do was keep an eye on Dave's place and let him know if we noticed anything. We were like a neighbourhood watch except we didn't call it that back then. I don't think we called it anything. Chris must have known we were onto him because Dave didn't have any problems after that apart from the usual ones that cockies had to put up with like outbreaks of facial eczema, drought or his best heading bitch coming on heat at the start of the muster, just the common everyday things.

With everything returning to normal Dave was able to relax a bit and get more involved with the club activities he enjoyed, especially the administration side of things which he had quite a flair for. On Friday afternoons it was my job to go into town and pick up a few crates for our Saturday night socials which had become a regular event and much looked forward to. We didn't have television back then or videos or casinos or nightclubs and the pubs closed at six o'clock so it gave us all the opportunity to get together and catch up on all the local gossip.

Going into town every Friday was still something of a hassle, especially in winter because the road wasn't up to much, but it gave me a chance to catch up on some shopping and as Ted and Sammy usually came along for the ride we'd make an outing of it. We'd shout ourselves to a movie and buy fish and chips for tea, eating them straight out of the newspaper on the way home. We always got back by 10 p.m. because Ted wasn't much of a night owl and insisted that ten o'clock was late enough for anybody.

After I dropped the beer off at the club rooms Ted would take a shortcut across the paddock to his place, then Sammy would ride home on his old Indian motorbike that had a torch tied on the handlebars because the headlight didn't work. That was our usual procedure but on this Friday night we didn't make it to the club rooms. Ted had dozed off but Sammy was wide awake and spotted it before I did. We had just turned onto the straight stretch of road between Cliff Roger's place and the club rooms when Sammy started pointing and yelling at the top of his voice. Poor old Ted nearly had a heart attack. He shot bolt upright staring about wildly and demanded to know what the bloody hell was going on.

Both Dave's house and woolshed were engulfed in flames and we could see somebody moving about. 'It can't be Dave,' Ted yelled out, 'he's spending the weekend in Wanganui.' None of us said anything but we guessed who that somebody was. Once through the gate I gunned the old Ford straight over the paddocks and caught the moving figure in the headlights. It had to be Chris and we were all sure of it, but it wasn't. It was his brother Wayne. He turned to face us just for a second but long enough for us to see that mole on his chin and when he took off there was no mistaking that ungainly pigeon-toed run of his. There was no time for discussion or anything else much. We were too late to fight the fire effectively with just a garden hose but while Ted raced back in the Ford to ring the fire brigade from Cliff Roger's place, Sammy and I managed to save a few of Dave's tools from the woolshed, but it wasn't much.

By the time the fire brigade arrived all they could do was damp down the ashes. They were pretty sure it was a case of arson and so were we. The police were called and we were asked to wait around to answer any questions they might have as we'd been first on the scene. We hung around for another two hours till the police showed up and by that time so had half the valley, including Dave. He was looking just like you'd expect a man to look who's just lost everything and was just as surprised as everybody else to hear that it was Wayne and not Chris we'd seen running away. 'I knew his brother hated my guts,' he said, 'but I didn't think Wayne held a grudge against me.'

The police got Sammy and me to go back into town with them and write out statements. By the time we'd done that and answered their questions all over again, it was daylight. We had breakfast at the railway cafe and later on that morning the police called round to speak to Wayne. We thought it was an open and shut case but things started to get a bit confused about then. The day after speaking to Wayne the police got hold of Ted, Sammy and me again and went over our statements with each of us so many times we were starting to wonder if we were the ones under suspicion. The thing that was worrying the police was our positive identification of Wayne, because he had a cast iron alibi.

According to the police Wayne claimed that he'd been in town at rehearsals with the amateur dramatic society he was involved with and hadn't left till after 11 p.m. After questioning all the other members of the cast who backed up Wayne's story they were at a standstill unless they could get us to admit we'd made a mistake. They tried telling us that it would have been easy for us to be wrong in our identification because it had been late at night and we'd only got a quick glimpse of whoever it was, but there had been no mistake. The three of us were sure of that so we stuck to our guns.

Over the next couple of months the police kept up their investigations, asking the same questions of everybody involved, but nothing came of it. Meanwhile Dave was struggling to get his life back on track. He had had some insurance money to fall back on but it was still going to be hard for him to keep going or even survive. Because we were the close-knit community I was telling you about, we all pitched in to help where we could. The hat was passed round, we raffled off wild pork at the pub, the ladies, bless their hearts, donated their bottled fruit, jams and pickles to be sold through the store and even the kids got in on the act, collecting bottles.

As soon as we got enough cash together I got the timber delivered on site, and to save money stipulated 'mixed grade' when ordering. This meant that the first grade stuff would have to be sorted from the second grade and the second grade from the boxing grade. But it wasn't a hard job and we had plenty of free labour. Even though it was opening weekend for duck shooting we had a good turnout on the day with everybody wanting to lend a hand. Profiles were being put up, foundations dug, weatherboards primed, ladies ran around with pots of tea and plates of scones — everybody was doing something, even if it didn't need doing.

Ted Thompson was wandering around aimlessly getting in the way and being abused for his troubles so I took his hurt feelings over to the pile of timber. 'You can have a go at sorting this lot out if you want, mate,' I said.

Ted looked at the timber like it was the crashed remains of a UFO. 'I'm not so sure if I can handle this job, Charger,' he said worriedly. 'I've never had much to do with wood; I wouldn't want to stuff things up.'

'You won't stuff things up, mate,' I promised. 'All you have to do is look at the end of each length. One black dot means it's first grade. Two for second and three for third, or boxing grade. Just separate it into three piles and that'll save a lot of time when we start knocking the frames together.'

Ted bent down and picked up a piece of four by two that had one black dot stamped on the end. 'So this is first grade,' he said.

'That's right,' I told him.

Ted picked up another piece and made a big show of carefully counting the three black dots. 'And this piece would be third grade then,' he stated, as though he'd discovered something the rest of the world hadn't.

'Right again, mate,' I said, but I could tell he was working up to something.

'Well I reckon it's a pretty stupid system,' he said.

'How do you figure that out, mate?'

Ted dug into his hip pocket for his tobacco tin and started rolling a smoke. 'If the only thing that separates first grade from third is a couple of black dots, what's to stop us putting three black dots on the whole bloody lot and telling the timber yard we only got third grade stuff, and that's all we're paying for.'

'Well it's not quite as simple as that, Ted,' I explained. 'You see, it's already been graded down at the yard, it just hasn't been sorted out. When they deliver it, all the grades and lengths are written on the docket which you sign for.'

'Fair enough,' Ted grinned, 'but I still reckon a man could cause a few problems if he had some black dots in his pocket.'

The thought of a mischievous Ted Thompson running around putting black dots on the ends of the timber had me grinning as well, but then I thought of something that wasn't so funny. Thinking back to the night of the fire I remembered how Ted, Sammy and I had identified Wayne by the mole on his chin and by the way he ran but it could just as easily have been Chris. All he had to do was put a mole on his chin or a black dot if you like with some of that make-up stuff they both used in their amateur dramatic groups and run off with his foot turned in.

And that was something else too. Why had Wayne, if he was really Chris, stayed around long enough to be seen? He had plenty of time to get away. Chris didn't have an alibi for the night of the fire. He said he was up at his possum camp and everybody believed him because we all knew he'd been spending a lot of time up there for quite a while. Besides that, all the suspicion had been directed towards Wayne.

I got Ted and Sammy together as soon as I could and went over everything with them piece by piece. 'It all fits,' Ted agreed. 'Chris would have known his brother was at rehearsals and so have a perfect alibi which would put him in the clear and I reckon being seen by us was part of his plan. He wanted us to identify him as his brother, otherwise like you say, Charger, why did he hang around? I think he timed it right too. He knew it was our habit to get back along that road around about ten o'clock at night.'

Discovering the truth didn't give us cause for celebration. In fact we were worried about our next move. Going to the police would mean a prison term for Chris and we didn't like the idea of doing that to one of our own, even if he was a bit of a ratbag. Ted and I discussed it at length and convinced each other that it would be better to let sleeping dogs lie, to let everything blow over. But if we kept quiet about Chris, the shadow of suspicion would always hang over Wayne because of the statements we'd made to the police. This was something that Sammy pointed out and we had to start rethinking everything all over again. What final decision would have been made between the three of us is something that will never be known.

Just two days later a couple of deerstalkers found Chris's body at the bottom of Cutler's Creek just a few minutes away from his possum camp. As near as anyone could tell he'd fallen about 30 metres and got smashed up quite badly. Death would have been instantaneous. The deerstalkers who found Chris's body reckoned they were going to have nightmares about it for the rest of their lives. They said it looked as though it had been there for at least a week and the rats had given it a fair bit of attention too. We didn't even like hearing about it. Terry and Fran arranged to have the funeral in town and apart from Wayne and some other close relatives who came over from Hamilton, no one else attended, namely because no one else was invited. Chris's death had been an accident, pure and simple, but for some reason or other Terry and Fran acted as if they held us responsible which, even allowing for their understandable grief, was still a bit over the top.

I think we were all hoping time would heal the rift, but time wasn't given a chance. Terry and Fran moved into town, bought a dairy and put their place up for sale. We didn't see anything of Wayne either, but rumour had it that he'd gone share milking on a property just outside Te Kuiti with a girl he'd met from over that way. It was always sad when anyone left the valley, but in this case it was all for the best. Terry, Fran and Wayne could get on with their lives and we could get on with ours. As time passed the events surrounding Chris's death and the fire became distant memories, just like they do in any community anywhere in the world.

In 1968 Ted Thompson went to live out his retirement in Turangi where he could fish the Major Jones pool on the Tongariro River every day just like he always said he would. Sammy, who by then was married with four kids, became one of our first deer farmers in the district, and I left to take a position as building consultant for a company operating in Hamilton. I barely had time enough to settle into my flash new office and get used to the company car when one of the first persons I happened to meet was Wayne Lester.

He was looking a bit older but so was I so I didn't mention it. He'd given up share milking and bought himself a commercial cleaning business and was doing okay on it. We were both thinking about the tragic event of almost twenty years before and as neither of us was going to mention it, conversation between us was so awkward as to be embarrassing. Wayne kept looking at his watch as if he had a pressing appointment. I was pretty sure it was just a ploy to get on his way but I gave him an opening anyway. 'You in a hurry, mate?' I said.

Wayne looked at his watch again for effect, and then lied through his teeth. 'Yes, as a matter of fact I am, Charger,' he said. 'I've got to pick the kids up from school. The wife usually does it but she's got a dentist's appointment. But we'll have to get together some time,' he added, trying to sound sincere.'

'Yeah, we'll do that some time, Wayne,' I said. I could have told him that there was no need for him to pick his kids up from school because it was the middle of the May holidays, but there was no point in embarrassing the bloke. Besides, as I watched him walk off to get lost among the crowd I realised he'd given me plenty to think about, like how come he didn't have that mole on his chin anymore? And why didn't he walk with his right foot turned in, like he always used to?

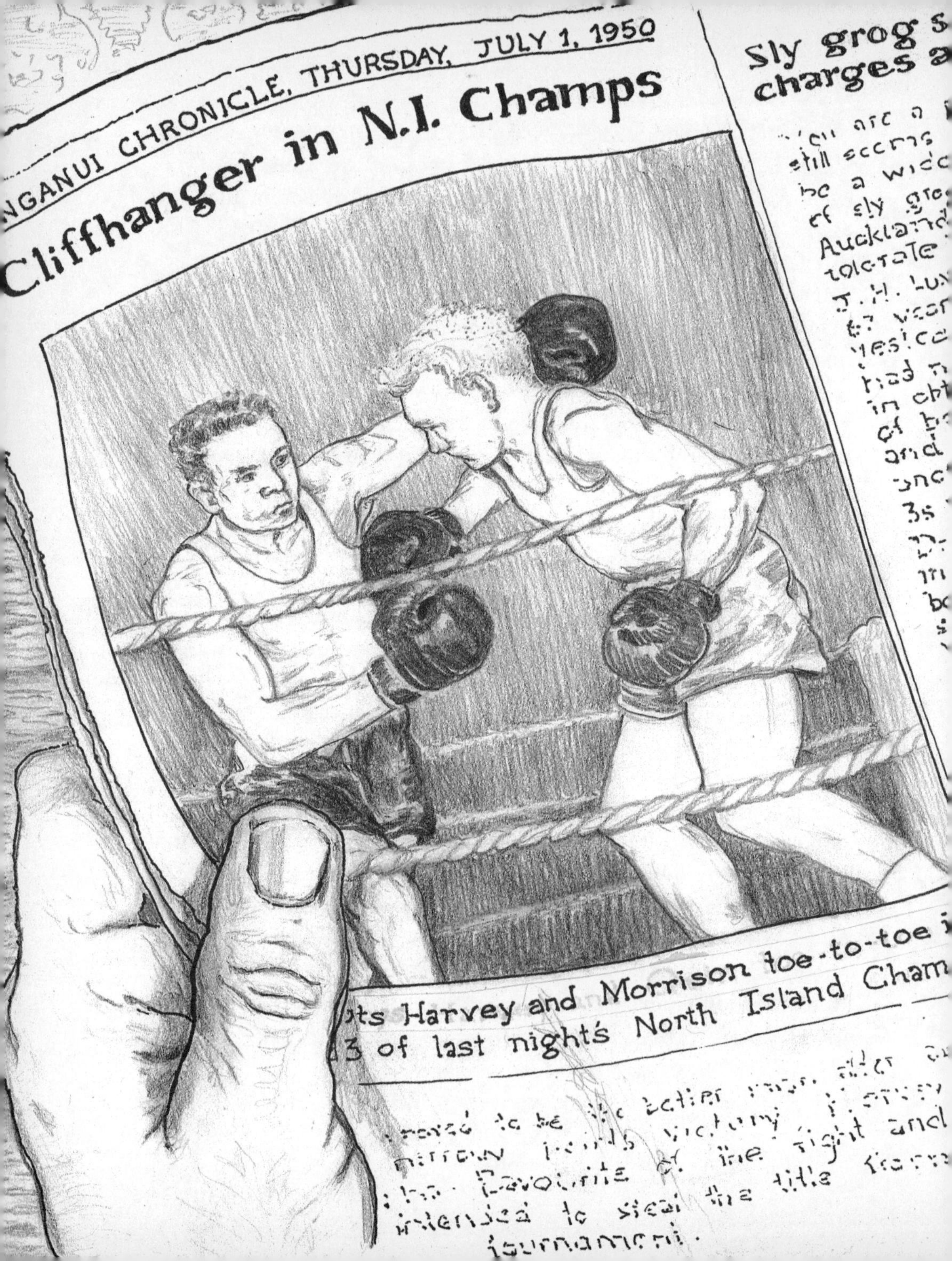
NGANUI CHRONICLE, THURSDAY, JULY 1, 1950
Cliffhanger in N.I. Champs
Sly grog
charges
Harvey and Morrison toe-to-toe
of last night's North Island

CHAPTER 7

Born to Win

There must have been over a hundred of us pighunters gathered outside the Riverside Tavern waiting for the winner of the biggest boar contest to be announced.

Most of us knew it was going to be Scott Harvey, but we hung around anyway. What with friends and family and curious passers-by stopping to have a look, the gathering had swelled to about three hundred, there was a festive air about and a good time was being had by all.

As expected, Scott took first prize for biggest boar and best set of tusks. Sammy Mita scored second equal with a bloke from Ohakune and Jack Philburn took third. This was the fourth contest we'd organised lately and Scott had taken first prize in all of them. The only time any of us could remember him having to take second best was when I'd scored a narrow points win over him two years before in the 1950 North Island Amateur Boxing Champs.

Like a true sportsman Scott had shaken my hand after the bout and with a good-natured grin had promised to turn the tables on me in the nationals. He might have done too, had he not sustained a shoulder injury playing rep rugby just one week before the scheduled bout.

The following year we both quit boxing because of other commitments so we never got round to having that return, which may have been a curse or a blessing depending on which way you looked at it. The fact that Scott Harvey was a winner was irrefutable. This was apparent right from our early days at primary school.

Miss Hammond, our teacher, had more of his paintings hanging on the classroom wall than the rest of us put together. He always got the best parts in school plays and pantomimes and always came away winning on sports days. Whenever teams were picked for football or cricket he was always captain of one or the other and it was his team that everybody wanted to be on because his team always won, even when it was made up with more girls than boys because we didn't have enough boys to go round.

During our teen years Scott carried on his winning way, representing the province in rugby, cricket and boxing, and still found time to run a three-dog team and score some of the biggest boars I've seen come out of the Wanganui River district.

I could never make up my mind whether Scott had a winning attitude because he was a winner or whether he was a winner because he had a winning attitude. The thought of failure never entered his head. Negativity was for other people, not him. On leaving school most of us took on apprenticeships or worked on the family farms with the intention of taking over the reins some time in the future, but not Scott. He swapped his motorbike for a pack horse along with a hundred traps and a .303 rifle and took to the Ruahine Ranges overlooking Dannevirke.

We didn't see him again till he came home for Christmas almost a year later. He'd filled out a bit and had the typical rugged tanned looks of the outdoorsman and something else too; his manner was different. It was as if he'd outgrown us. Maybe the lonely demanding life he'd chosen had forced him to mature early. Whatever it was, we didn't like it. It made us feel as though we were kids talking to a grown-up.

He was still a winner though, that much hadn't changed. In the ten months he'd been away trapping possums he'd made more money than any of us were likely to earn in the next five years. I told my old man that I was quitting my carpentry apprenticeship and heading for the bush too. He wasn't too keen on that idea: 'Like hell you are. You'll serve your time first, then you can go bush and play silly beggars.'

'But he's making a mint, Dad,' I argued.

'He might be, but what's he going to do when he's too old to tramp the hills? Answer me that,' my father demanded.

'With the kind of money he's making, retire in the lap of luxury at 35,' I told him. But it was no use. Parents in those days had fixed ideas about learning a trade and things like that.

While Scott had been away a few of us locals had got together and formed a rod and gun club. We originally intended it to be a pighunting club but we were only a small community so to help make up the numbers we invited the deerstalkers and trout fishermen to join. This brought the membership up to 34. Meetings were held once a month at the community hall and the interest generated by club members never wavered.

That first year Mark Berry had won the club's deerstalking trophy with a massive 14-point Red, Jack Philburn had taken the angling section with a 14-pound brownie, and a 300-pound boar had been good enough for me to win the pighunter's award. As soon as Scott heard about the club he paid his subs and just to show he hadn't lost his touch, went straight out and scored a Captain Cooker that dragged the needle down to 307 lb 4 oz. A week later he returned to his camp in the Ruahines and life carried on as usual for us mere mortals living in the valley.

He came home again the following Christmas with a bulging bank account, a dozen or so trophy-sized lower jaws and a 14-point Red deer head that pushed Mark's effort into second place. He told me that he'd be trapping a bit closer to home from then on: 'It's not as if I'll be stepping on anyone's toes, Charger,' he explained over a couple of beers at the Riverside pub one Saturday afternoon. 'The only other trapper working the district is Darcy Knapps and I reckon there's more than enough country for the two of us.'

Scott was right about that and working close to home he was able to rejoin the football team, which welcomed him back with open arms, and take up boxing again for the YMCA. Nothing succeeds like success and Scott Harvey was a living monument to that. Apart from his one loss to me in the North Island champs, coming first was as natural to him as breathing.

After completing my apprenticeship as per Father's orders, I thought seriously about going bush and playing 'silly beggars'. A friend of a friend whose second cousin was married to someone who worked for the Department of Internal Affairs pulled a few strings and got me signed on as a deer culler. The job was nothing like I expected: cold, damp and lonely for most of the time, but I lasted out two seasons, which was two seasons longer than the vast majority of those who chanced their arm. I learned a few things about crossing rivers and lighting fires in the wet and baking bread in a camp oven, and even managed to drop enough deer to keep the Department happy while I was at it.

My return to the valley went unheralded. I don't think anyone even noticed I'd been away. The football team said they'd phone me if they needed me and when I called in at the gym Ike Farley, my trainer and mentor, asked me why I hadn't been to training lately. 'Have you had a touch of the flu, mate?' he enquired.

This after a year's absence and from a man who had predicted I would be the next Empire champion. (I found out years later that he told everybody that, cunning old sod.) Things like that can deflate a bloke. My one consolation was the roll of skin money acquired through sweat and toil. It would be enough to keep me going while plans to start a building business were put into effect.

There was every reason to have confidence in the venture. The only other builder in the immediate district was old George Cathaway and he was due to retire any time. There was plenty of work about. Round about the same time as this Scott decided to give the trapping game away. He moved into town with his savings and bought a truck for the purpose of starting up his own carrier service. A year and a half later I was just starting to show a profit. This had been achieved through working a 10-hour day and taking only one weekend off in every month to go pighunting. It was just enough to prevent me and the dogs suffering withdrawal symptoms.

Scott had by this time purchased another four trucks, and had a team of drivers working for him along with a secretary and an accountant. He was making more money than a stockbroker and seemed to have unlimited time for recreational pursuits. If he wasn't fishing the river then he was hunting the hills above it. He even had the time not to mention the wherewithal to shout himself a trip to Canada for a moose hunt. Naturally he got one, and not just your normal everyday moose either. His had to be a Canadian record.

While I had to have a minimum of two referrals from upstanding long-serving members just to be eligible to join the Workingmen's Club, Scott was being pandered to by members of the Rotary, the Young Lions, the Druids, the Freemasons, the Gentlemen's Club and the Royal Order of Buffaloes all eager to sign him on. Scott Harvey had come a long way and outgrown us in every direction. He hardly bothered with our rod and gun club any more and the hunting and fishing to be had in the Wanganui River district no longer interested him.

With his big-time business associates he hunted the Kaimanawa Ranges for his sika deer and the Southern Alps for thar and chamois. It came as something of a surprise when he showed up at our New Year's Eve social. There was nothing wrong with our socials, but compared to what he'd grown accustomed to they were a bit on the rough and ready side, typical of those times in rural communities, what with the ladies bringing plates and the blokes all putting in for the keg, the band almost invariably made up of local talent whose repertoire would seldom exceed half a dozen old time tunes and the atmosphere reeking of Christmas present hair oil, perfume and aftershave.

Scott had a lady friend with him who he introduced as Lana. He'd never had trouble attracting the girls, but Lana was something special as far as looks went. Honey blonde hair, blue eyes and the kind of figure that most women would kill for. I didn't think much of her manner though. You could tell she regarded us as just a bunch of country hicks. She thought the decorations in the hall were 'tatty', the band a 'dead loss' and the spread of savouries and sandwiches put on by the ladies not worth leaving her seat for. Scott had the cheek to make excuses for us, as if we needed excusing. 'You must remember, darling,' he soothed, 'they're only simple country folk born to the land.'

'And we don't forget our roots, either,' I snarled loud enough for everybody in our corner of the hall to hear.

For just a second or so Scott's eyes glared angrily at me. I thought we were about to have our return match but he calmed down and mumbled something about not meaning to offend anybody. They left shortly after, and I don't think anybody minded — or perhaps just one person: Frank Peters, a local lad, who though only sixteen was big for his age and had the manner and the appearance of an older man. It was no secret that he liked older women and he and Lana had had a couple of dances together. Frank cornered me later in the night to ask me about an apprenticeship. I told him I'd think about it. Apart from his brief appearance to collect the prize money for the winner of our fourth localised pighunting contest, we never saw anything of Scott for months and even then it was only his wedding photo in the local paper.

He'd married Lana and none of us had been invited to the wedding. There were a few noses put out of joint over that, not least of all Sammy Mita's, Scott's best friend in what we were all referring to as the 'old days'.

'He used to be a mate, Charger. Now he acts like he doesn't want to know us.'

'Not to worry, Sammy,' I replied, 'We'll get our own back by not inviting him and that stuck-up wife of his to our New Year's Eve social.'

It was meant as a joke, but Sammy wasn't in the mood for any Morrison humour right then. Scott and Lana had a month's honeymoon in Tahiti and about a week after they got back Sammy and I spotted them in town just as we were leaving Dalgety's. They'd been on a shopping spree going by the number of parcels they were carrying and were in the middle of a serious disagreement about something. Lana was hissing and spitting like a ferret caught in a gin trap and Scott, looking very subdued and embarrassed at the scene she was creating, was trying to smooth things over by not answering back.

She all but threw the parcel she was carrying onto the back seat of the brand new Buick they'd had shipped out from the States before seating herself in the passenger side and slamming the door shut. The look of utter hopelessness on Scott's face as they drove away was something to behold. He looked anything but a winner right then.

Sammy muttered something about the honeymoon being well and truly over. No comment. I had other things to attend to. The small one-man building business I'd started just two years before was starting to grow. I took on an apprentice and a labourer to help with the workload which made it possible for me and the dogs to get out every weekend, and I'd paid cash for a mint condition 1948 Ford V8 15-cwt truck. Me and the dogs had never had it so good.

The bush was crawling with pigs. For a total of 119 days' actual hunting that year, 204 pigs of various sizes were accounted for by yours truly in the company of my two holders Grab and Mitch and finder Mike. This figure does not include the three-quarter-grown boar that I'd bowled over with the Ford driving home from Sammy's place one night or the two 80-pound porkers I shot from the back porch while they were helping themselves to a free feed out of Mum's vegie garden. It does, however, include the boar that beat the club record held by Scott Harvey.

It was a good day, that was. The only damper on the proceedings were the injuries suffered by Mitch who always showed more guts than sense. He needed a total of 44 stitches and a series of glucose and saline injections to combat shock and blood loss. The hair-raising ride into the vet's hadn't done him any favours either, but he recovered. I'd had a good run with dogs, all things considered. Mitch was still getting ripped often enough to be on first name terms with the vet but I hadn't lost a dog and was using the same pack I'd started with.

Grab was starting to slow down with age, which was a bit of a worry, as quite often Mitch would arrive on the scene well ahead and go in on his own, which contributed to his injury rate. I put the word about that I was looking for another holder and got a call from a bloke in town. The dog belonged to his son who'd moved to Auckland and wouldn't have any more use for it. The old bloke, 'Call me 'Arry,' reckoned that Boss was too good a dog to make a pet out of, and invited me round to have a look.

I found Harry's place without too much trouble in spite of the complicated directions he had given me. I liked the look of Boss: part cattle dog, part bull terrier with a bit of whippet thrown in for speed, smooth coated and jet black in colour apart from a patch of white on his chest. The four-inch scar on his right shoulder told its own story. Harry wouldn't take any money for Boss but said I could drop him off a dozen next time I was in town. I promised I would, and I did.

Before heading back, I thought I'd catch up on a bit of shopping. I bumped into Scott, quite literally, while he was coming out and I was going into the Farmers Trading Store. I don't think either of us was particularly thrilled about seeing each other, but the meeting was unavoidable. I told him he was looking well, which was an outright lie, because he looked bloody awful, as if he hadn't slept for a month and was recovering from a bad case of the 'flu.

I asked him how things were and he said, 'Fine,' which was another lie, but I didn't know it at the time. We stood there feeling awkward in each other's company for a few minutes, making strained small talk before giving each other the old line about having to rush off because of pressing business, which wasn't the truth either, and we both knew it.

I picked up a few things I needed, paid the girl behind the counter and was all set to leave when a tap on the shoulder had me turning round and shaking hands with old Ernie Bruce. He'd owned the farm next to ours when I was still at school but had been forced to retire from the land because of a crook ticker. It was good to see the old bloke again and he seemed just as happy to see me, so heading off to the public bar of the Criterion Hotel to catch up on old times seemed the most natural thing to do.

I told Ernie about my building business and the pighunting contests we'd been having and all about the rod and gun club and somehow that bit about me holding the club record for the biggest boar slipped out during the course of the conversation. 'You can shout me a double rum, if I'm going to have to listen to you skite, young Morrison,' Ernie grumbled.

He was only joking, but I shouted him one anyway. 'Have you seen much of Scott since he moved into town?' I asked, to keep the conversation going.

Ernie pulled a face as if he'd taken a mouthful of brake fluid. 'Me and Mum have invited him and his wife over for tea a few times,' Ernie admitted, 'but they always say they're too busy. Between you and me, Charger, I don't think there's too much in the way of marital bliss in the Harvey household.' Ernie took another sip of his rum before going on. 'It's only rumour of course, but the story is that Lana is spending money faster than Scott can make it and he's been borrowing heavily. He's also having problems getting business since another carrier service opened up in competition and to top it all off there's been a few whispers about Lana not being above a bit of hanky-panky with some of the drivers.'

I shouted Ernie another rum and promised to call in on him and 'Mum' and drove back with plenty to think about. I called in to see how things were progressing with Bob Sutton's new implement shed. I'd left the boys to it while I'd gone in to pick up Boss. Frank Peters, my apprentice, had all the timber laid out in respective sizes and lengths and was slapping a coat of used sump oil on some six by one boxing. He was a good worker, was Frank, though he had one major fault that I always found annoying. Whether it was setting out the profiles or framing or hanging a door, he'd always forget to square things up and usually ended up in some kind of bother because of it. 'You can't fit a square window frame into an out-of-square hole, Frank,' I must have told him a thousand times; but he was getting the hang of it and more than willing to put in plenty of overtime, though heaven knows what he was doing with his money. I guessed he was saving up for a flash car or something. On the other hand Ray Goode, the labourer I'd taken on, wasn't living up to his name. He'd hardly made any impression on digging the foundations when he should have had the job half done at least. Ray would do a passable day's work when I was around to keep an eye on him but he couldn't be trusted on his own and I was having serious thoughts about letting him go.

Bob called down and asked me to come up to the house, he had a few things he wanted to discuss. As soon as I walked in the door, Bob's wife Irene put the kettle on and Bob got straight to the point. 'Seeing as you're building our new implement shed, Charger, Irene and me were wondering if you'd like to build our new home as well. My grandfather built this place and I don't think it's going to remain standing for much longer,' Bob laughed, 'and besides, I promised Irene a new house when we got married, and that was ten years ago.'

Bob went on to explain how he could provide some of the timber from his father's mill and for extra labour I could make use of any one of the two shepherds he had on the place. I told Bob I'd get back to him with a quote. Being a Friday, Frank and Ray knocked off early, so I got home with enough daylight left to give Boss a run with his new mates. There was a chance of being caught out in the dark with Mike being something of a long range finder, but this time he sussed out a rank old boar at the bottom of a gully just twenty minutes from our boundary fenceline.

Boss and Mitch arrived at the scene together and took hold of an ear each and laid back hard against the boar's flanks. Grab arrived at the same time as me and looked a bit put out at not having anything to do. He was breathing heavier than me too, and trying not to show it. I stuck the boar, an old battler who showed all the signs of having spent a hard winter, and inspected the tusks. They were a passable pair.

As soon as we got back I fed the dogs, had a shave and shower and made a phone call. Ten minutes later I was gunning the Ford out to Sammy Mita's place, whistling a tune that I didn't know the name of and feeling better than I had in months. It had been a good day, what with scoring a new holder, another trophy, being offered the biggest contract to date; and the day wasn't over yet.

Sammy's sister, Leah, who just happened to be one of the best lookers in the district, had agreed to go to the pictures with me that night. Sitting in the 1/9d seats sharing a packet of Jaffas isn't exactly the kind of thing that would put a young joker into orbit these days, but this was 1954, and a bloke had to start somewhere.

I gave the dogs another run on the weekend and came to grips with my first ever barrow. I also found time to go over the plans of Bob's new house. Taking into account the materials and labour he was supplying, I put in a quote for three and a half thousand pounds which included the implement shed and one extra haybarn. Bob was happy with that, and we shook hands on it.

As the job progressed Frank kept right on improving, but Ray got steadily worse. He was either turning up late or not at all, had endless excuses for knocking off early and he had long stopped giving a fair day's work for a better than fair day's pay. It was time to have a quiet word with Mr Goode. 'If you're not happy working for me, Ray, maybe it's best you finish up.'

Ray stood there looking at the ground like a crestfallen boy who'd just broken his favourite toy. 'Listen, mate,' I said in a friendlier tone, 'I don't like the idea of sacking anybody, and if you've got some kind of a problem that's affecting your work, then tell me about it and maybe we can do something.'

It took Ray a while but finally he admitted to having a gambling problem and that he had debts amounting to more than five hundred pounds and was in breach of a court order to repay, which meant there was every chance of him doing a stretch inside. Would I lend him the money?

Lending money to a compulsive gambler is like putting an alcoholic in charge of a bottle store — not a wise move. I told Ray he could have his job for as long as he wanted it, provided he gave me a fair go, and that I would make arrangements on his behalf to pay off his debts. That was as far as I was prepared to go, which I honestly thought was fair under the circumstances, but he didn't seem very satisfied with it.

He sloped off back to the job but didn't seem to be working any harder than he was before. Bob came down later in the day to see if I needed anything and gave me a thousand pounds all in five pound notes wrapped up in a canvas bag that had BNZ stencilled on it in black ink. 'Progress payment, Charger,' Bob explained.

I hadn't asked for a progress payment, so it was a pleasant surprise. 'Thanks, Bob, but wouldn't it have been easier to write out a cheque?'

Bob shook his head. 'You don't want to go writing out cheques, mate, otherwise people get to know how much money a man's got, and we can't have that now, can we?'

'You're a hard man, Bob,' I grinned. 'I'll write you out a receipt.'

'No hurry,' Bob assured. 'You can bring it up to the house when you knock off for lunch.'

I put the money in the glove box of the Ford and thought no more about it.

The morning flew by and it wasn't until Frank had boiled the Thermette for a brew that I realised it was lunchtime. I grabbed the receipt book and went up to the house with the intention of just dropping off the receipt and rejoining the boys for a cuppa, but Irene put the kibosh on that. She placed a freshly baked apple pie on the table and a jug of fresh cream and insisted I have at least one helping. Not wanting to offend the lady, I had at least three.

When I got back to the site with my belt loosened by two notches, Frank had already restarted on the framing. I had a quick look around. 'Where's Ray got to, Frank?'

'He's just gone down to the store for a packet of smokes,' Frank answered, without looking up or missing a stroke with his hammer. An hour went by and Ray still hadn't returned. I figured even if his car had broken down he'd had ample time to walk back. I glanced over at the Ford and noticed the passenger side door was slightly ajar. I could have sworn I'd closed it.

'Has anybody been into the Ford for anything, Frank?' I enquired.

Frank stopped to scratch himself behind the ear and thought about it for a couple of seconds. 'Oh, yeah,' he remembered. 'Ray helped himself to a Band-aid for a cut finger just as we knocked off for lunch.'

For Ray to get a Band-aid meant that he needed the first aid kit which was always kept in the glove box of the Ford. I had a sick feeling that had nothing to do with apple pie and cream as I walked over to the Ford. The first aid kit was lying on the passenger seat with half the contents tipped out and the BNZ cash bag was lying on the floor — empty.

I was numb with shock, not wanting to believe it. I raced up to the house and while Bob rang the police, Irene stood around wringing her hands and I paced around having murderous thoughts about Mr Goode and wringing his neck. An elderly sergeant and a young constable came out and took all the particulars and said they'd let me know when they had something.

Weeks went by without me hearing a damn thing about Ray Goode or my thousand quid. The police were sympathetic but there wasn't a hell of a lot they could do. Ray had vanished without trace. It wouldn't have been hard to do back then. He could have lost himself in any one of a thousand back country jobs, where questions were seldom asked.

It took me a while to come right. A thousand quid was a hell of a lot of money to lose in 1954. Leah offered to pay me into the pictures every time we went out, which was something. We were seeing quite a bit of each other. The other consolation was of course the pighunting. Running the dogs and doing battle with the tuskers of the Wanganui River district was in a funny way restorative.

I managed to secure two or three fairly lucrative contracts and was just starting to make headway again when I saw Scott's bankruptcy notice in the paper. I drove over to offer something in the way of moral support, but the house was empty. One of his neighbours told me that Scott had moved over to Taupo, he and Lana had separated and the house was being sold to pay off his creditors.

Bad news travels fast, and when the club got to hear about Scott's misfortune there was a lot of sympathy expressed, because in spite of everything, Scott had been one of us. For my birthday Leah bought me a Smithfield cross that answered to the name of Mate. She'd picked it up from a breeder in Ohakune who used to hunt with her dad. I was rapt. 'Been after a Smithfield for years,' I told her.

She wouldn't tell me how much she paid for the dog, because it was a gift, and it wasn't polite for me to ask anyway. To cover my embarrassment I asked her what she wanted for her birthday. She pretended to think about it for a few moments. 'An engagement ring would be nice.'

Bloody hell!

Mate was only a young dog without experience but after just a few runs he started to shape up nicely. Grab had slowed to the point of embarrassment but if I left him behind he'd invariably sulk and pick a fight with one of the others as soon as we got back, and would only cease when threatened with a stick.

I ended up letting him tag along just to keep the peace. He was always more of a hindrance than a help but it was still a sad day for me when he finally succumbed to old age. In his prime Grab had been one of the best. He'd never held back or lost a boar once he'd taken hold in all the years we'd hunted together.

Leah and I got engaged on her birthday and were married three months later. We had an open air reception with Sammy and Uncle Willy doing the hangi and those in attendance numbered 34 from my side of the family and 187 from hers — thank God only half of them could make it.

We had none of the problems that newlyweds are supposed to have adjusting to married life and for a while we thought maybe there was something wrong with us. The next five years went by and there were few changes in the valley. Frank served his time and despite the fact that I was willing to offer him a generous salary to stay on, he said he had plans about moving to Australia. He didn't seem to want to talk about it; he sounded pretty vague actually. I took on another apprentice who was turning out all right, and then finally got word regarding Ray Goode. He'd run his car off the road, killing himself outright and injuring the other passenger in the car somewhere up towards Whangarei. Not a very satisfactory conclusion and if I hadn't already, I finally said goodbye to my thousand quid. I couldn't feel any animosity towards the bloke; whatever sins he'd committed in life, he'd paid the ultimate price.

Frank came round to see me just before setting sail for Australia. I had a few of the boys around from the club, which seemed to cramp his style a bit. I thought perhaps he was going to hit me up for a reference or something. He had a couple of quick beers then we shook hands and wished each other goodbye and good luck.

Membership numbers for the rod and gun club stayed much the same and competitions were still creating interest, though we noticed the percentage of pighunters from the towns and cities was on the increase, as was the use of bailing dogs as opposed to holders.

As ongoing secretary I kept all the club records going back to our first official meeting. Reading through the old minutes, the motions forwarded and seconded, and by whom, was something I had never tired of. We had in a way created our own history. The name Scott Harvey would sometimes appear and I would spare a moment for a one-time friend and wonder what had ever happened to him.

A newspaper article sent to us by Stuart Broadmore, elected president of a hunting club in Hawke's Bay, provided something of a clue. The article, headed 'Boys bring home the bacon', had a photograph depicting a 374-pound boar with a pair of local hunters and their dogs proudly posing alongside. A brief account of the hunt accompanied the photograph, but what caught my eye were the words 'This monster beats the previous club record held by S. Harvey, by more than 50 pounds.'

A toll call through to Stuart confirmed that it was the same Scott Harvey, and Stuart was sure he was still in the area even though he hadn't been to any club meetings for some time.

The drive over to Hastings was pleasant enough, though that bit through the Manawatu Gorge was a bit hairy in the old Ford. I found Stuart's house easily enough, and after a brew followed his directions out to a metal road that ran off the Napier-Taupo highway, just north of Te Pohue. 'It's a white weatherboard place with a red roof. You'll find it easily enough,' Stuart had promised.

And he was right about that. It was the only house for miles around. There was some washing on the line and I noticed four dogs of the type that could only be owned by a pighunter, neatly housed in kennels behind the homestead. The front door opened and a bloke in faded blue jeans and a well-worn bush shirt stepped out onto the verandah. He was a little older, but looking a whole lot fitter than the last time I saw him. 'G'day, Scott, good to see you again, mate.'

Scott stood there staring unbelievingly. 'Well I'll be damned. Charger Morrison. I don't believe it!'

He rushed over and shook my hand hard enough to dislocate my shoulder. 'Well I'll be damned!' he repeated. 'Come on inside, mate, and meet Claire — that's the wife. We've got a son too; only a year old, but he's going to be a pighunter, mark my words. Have you had tea yet? When did you get here? How did you find out where I lived?'

Claire came to the door wiping her hands on a tea towel and told Scott to shut up, though in a nice way. 'Give the man a chance to get his breath, hon.'

'Yeah, sure, sorry about that. Meet the wife, Charger. Claire, this is my old mate, Charger Morrison. Charger, this is my wife, Claire.'

'G'day.'

'Nice to meet you, Charger. Have a seat and I'll put the kettle on.'

Over numerous cups of tea, followed by a roast dinner, followed by more tea, Scott and I talked long into the night. We had a lot to catch up on. Scott told me how, after separating from Lana and dealing with the bankruptcy, he'd come over to the Hawke's Bay more or less to start again. He built himself a hut in the Ahimanawa Ranges and went back to possuming. 'I should never have left it, Charger,' Scott confessed. 'A man's got to stick to what he's good at, especially when he's happy doing it.'

I couldn't argue with that. 'Have you ever heard anything about Lana?' I asked out of curiosity, making sure that Claire was out of earshot. Scott chuckled but without humour. 'Not a lot, mate,' he admitted. 'After we separated, we never saw each other again. Everything was handled by the lawyers. I heard some rumour about her conning somebody out of a pile of money and doing a runner up to Auckland. I've heard the odd rumour since, the latest being that she's gone over to Aussie to live with her parents. I'm not too worried about her; she'll find another mug to spend money on her.'

'Did you ever catch up with Ray Goode?' he asked.

I shook my head. 'No mate, not really. He caught up with himself. Ran his car off the road and killed himself.'

'Saved you doing the job for him, eh, Charger?'

'I don't know whether I would have actually killed him, but I think I would have made a hospital case out of him if I'd caught up with him. I was ropeable with him pulling a stunt like that. Especially after I was prepared to help him.'

I would have liked to take Scott up on his invitation to stay for a few days and have a crack at the Ahimanawa tuskers that Scott reckoned would have eaten my dogs for breakfast, but work commitments dictated otherwise. I was sorry to leave after such a brief visit and both Scott and Claire seemed genuinely sorry to see me go. We promised to keep in touch (we still do) and I drove away the next morning knowing that Scott Harvey was a winner again.

He wasn't driving a late model Buick any more, he got around in an old Vauxhall sedan, and he'd swopped his flash house on Snob Hill for a modest bungalow out in the sticks, but he was happy and totally at peace with what he had. Anyone who has that is a winner.

Just before Christmas that year I got a letter with an Australian postmark on it. It was from Frank. It was a fairly brief letter. 'Dear Charger,' it read. 'It's time to square things up. I'm meeting somebody tonight though she doesn't know it yet. She wasn't worth stealing for and I don't suppose she's worth doing a long stretch inside for, either. But like you were always telling me, things have to be squared up. Regards, Frank.'

I read the letter through several times. It took a while for everything to sink in. I couldn't really believe it, maybe I didn't want to, but the enclosed cheque for a thousand pounds confirmed it.

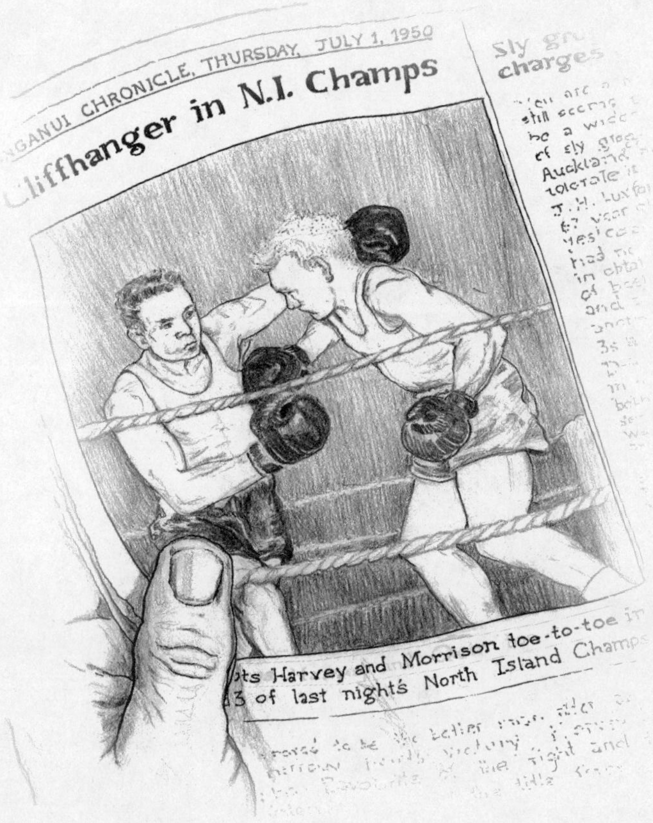
NGANUI CHRONICLE, THURSDAY, JULY 1, 1950
Cliffhanger in N.I. Champs
charges
Harvey and Morrison toe-to-toe in
of last night's North Island Champs

CHAPTER 8

What's in a Name?

When Garry Epping called in to my office looking for a job in that second week of September 1957, I was so short handed and snowed under with work, I was tempted to give him a start in spite of his record. I'd known Garry and his mum since they'd moved into the district ten years before when Garry was only eight years old, and right from day one he'd hardly ever been out of trouble.

Most of his problems seemed to stem from his school days where, despite showing a high degree of intelligence, his reading and writing levels never advanced beyond that of a seven-year-old. By the time he was fifteen they'd finally discovered that Garry had a form of dyslexia which affected his ability to read letters the way most of us do. To Garry words or letters always looked the opposite way round but because he didn't know any different it was hard for him to explain it to other people.

Ted Thompson's sister Betty had had some experience in teaching kids with problems like Garry's and kindly offered to help out, but by that time Garry decided he'd had a gutsful of teachers, school and everything else associated with the education system. At just fifteen years of age he left home and got a job on a dairy farm in the

Waikato district then left that to do a two-year stint as a deer culler in the Kaimanawa Range. So taken all round you could say Garry Epping had learnt a thing or two by the time he came knocking on my door looking for a job, and maybe that's why I agreed to give him a trial even though I sensed he still had something of a chip on his shoulder.

After only a month my fears were dispelled as Garry proved to be a hell of a worker who only had to be shown how to do something the once. Everything was going sweet, in fact, when I almost spoilt it by unintentionally humiliating the young bloke. It was pay day and I was handing out the wage packets when I noticed Garry had never signed the wage book. It was only a small thing but it had to be put right in case some overzealous employee from the Inland Revenue Department starting poking his nose round and asking silly questions.

Garry was in the smoko shed having afternoon tea with my other two employees, Dave Robbie and Archie Falloon, when I pointed it out, bit of a dumb move that. 'Just put your signature alongside where I've written your name, Garry,' I smiled. 'That'll keep the tax boys off my back.'

Garry's face flushed with embarrassment and I realised my mistake. I took the book back quickly. 'What the hell, Garry,' I said, 'it doesn't have to be done right now. We'll fix it up later.' I was still feeling bad about it two hours later when the boys knocked off for the day, so I was relieved when Garry followed me into the office with the offer to 'fix things up'. I handed over the wage book again, showed Garry where to sign and watched in amazement as he laboriously wrote out the word 'Oxo' alongside his name. I was determined not to say anything but that's not easy to do when somebody uses a gravy brand for a signature.

It was good to see Garry smiling which meant he could see the funny side of it too. 'I can write my name,' he explained, 'but most of the time I get the "g" or the "r" round the wrong way so I write "Oxo" instead because you can't get those letters round the wrong way. It still comes out right provided I remember to put the "x" in the middle.'

As I could more or less follow Garry's reasoning and didn't think it would matter all that much anyway, I let him carry on signing the wage book as 'Oxo' though I didn't let anyone else see it. Over the next couple of months the young bloke showed he could handle any job from digging foundations through to knocking up framing. He definitely had the makings of a good tradesman except for his problem of not being able to read, which meant he would never be able to follow written specifications. I knew he wasn't too keen on taking Betty Thompson up on her offer but just before Christmas that year I was able to twist his arm a bit. Garry had developed an interest in pighunting which occupied all his free time and half of mine. At every smoko break he'd pester me with questions regarding wild pigs. He wanted to know everything about them: their habits, life spans, breeding cycles, likely locations in relation to the seasons, how many dogs made up the best pack, were holders better than bailers or vice versa, etc., etc.

In the end I gave the dogs a run in the bush behind Bob Hartnell's place and took Garry along for the ride. It was a well-known piece of bush that most pighunters avoided like the plague. Rugged to the extreme, a man seemed to spend most of his time walking uphill and pushing his way through ferns coarse enough to cut through clothing, and the boars were so mean they used to attack the dogs. I honestly thought a day out there would knock some of the enthusiasm out of him but that was another dumb move on my part. Garry stuck his first pig that day. A mean 140-pound razor-back which drew blood on all three of my dogs. They had him cornered up against a rata which had fallen across a dirty little creek at the bottom of a dirty little gully. Everything looked straightforward at first, but that boar knew his stuff.

He was quicker on his feet than Carl Lewis and packed more punch than Mike Tyson. He was cunning with it too. He kept himself backed up against the rata so the dogs couldn't get in from behind and fought them on his terms. The dogs were working themselves up into a frenzy and as soon as one of them got too close he'd rush out flashing the ivory then retreat back to the rata before any of them could do anything. It was starting to look as though this game would go on for ever unless I could climb above and use the rifle, though that didn't look like much of an option.

The sides of the gully were almost vertical and there wasn't a lot of scrub or anything to hang onto. I started to pick my way up and around as best I could. My feet kept slipping out from under me and almost everything I grabbed hold of came away smelling of rot. Eventually I got far enough around to be above the boar but couldn't do anything because I was too busy hanging on. Right then the boar charged out to have a go at my finder Meg and that's when my holders Grab and Skipper pulled off a move that was nothing short of brilliant. As the boar lunged at Meg, Grab and Skipper scrambled up the sides of the gully then dropped down on either side of the boar. A classical pincer movement perfectly timed. They had a good hold but in the close confines of the gully were getting knocked round something wicked.

I couldn't get down in a hurry without risking a broken leg and was already counting how many stitches the dogs were going to need when Garry decided to get in on the act. I'd forgotten all about him. He stepped in, flipped the boar over, stuck it and was wiping the blade clean on its rump before I knew what had happened.

After that episode pighunting ceased to be an interest to Garry; it became an obsession. While most of the other young blokes in his age group were thinking about fast cars and pretty girls his only ambition was to get his own pack of dogs, but that was going to cost him. The asking price for a good pair of holder/bailers back then was anything up to three months' wages and a man could name his own figure for a reliable finder. Poor Garry was crestfallen. He'd spent most of his savings on a Morris 8 that still needed a fair bit of work, and was only just making ends meet. I was training a couple of young dogs, Missy and Bruce, that were showing a lot of promise and had a couple of hunts to their credit, so I told Garry he could have them for free provided he took reading and writing lessons from Betty Thompson. 'I'm not trying to run your life, mate,' I said, 'but if you're going to succeed in any trade you've got to know how to read and write. Even if you stick to labouring jobs or farm work there will still be times when it will be necessary.'

Garry still wasn't keen on the idea but he finally agreed to three lessons a week, which made me and Betty Thompson happy, and went home with two potentially good pig dogs, which made him happy. Over the next five months Garry ran his dogs every weekend and did okay with them too. He also stuck to his part of the bargain by religiously attending his evening lessons with Betty Thompson. Whether it was the one-on-one instruction, Betty's teaching skills, Garry's willingness to learn or a combination of all three is anybody's guess, but Garry's rate of improvement was more than noticeable.

He liked to show it off a bit too, which was understandable. If he was anywhere near the office when the phone rang he'd snatch it up before anybody else got a chance and write down the message. He also made a big show of reading the specifications listed with whichever job we were on. I would have been happy to keep Garry on but work started getting scarce as we headed into the winter of 1958. Winter's never a good time for the building game and most contractors expect things to slacken off a bit but this was the worst I'd ever seen. I barely had three months' work in reserve and nothing new was coming in. Having to lay Garry off was one of the hardest things I'd ever had to do as an employer, but the young bloke took it on the chin like a trooper. 'No worries, Mr Morrison,' he said. 'I've been thinking about having a go at the possums anyway and this looks like a good time to start.'

Garry didn't have any traps and didn't know much about the game but I was able to help out which made me feel a bit better. I had a hundred traps and peg boards hanging up in my old man's woolshed and the bush behind his place held a reasonably high possum population. There was also an old musterer's hut on the bush edge which Garry could use. Nothing flash but it was warm and dry.

That weekend I helped Garry clean up the hut and drag enough firewood out of the bush to keep him going for a while. I also gave him a demonstration in sleeve skinning using a few possums we'd picked up off the road, showed him how to stretch the skins out on the peg boards and helped him lay out his trap line. I kept a fair bit of distance between the traps in case they had to be moved and set the line out in a big rough circle so that he wouldn't have to cover the same ground twice. There wasn't a whole lot more I could do after that so I left the young bloke to it, but not before warning him about the Wheeler brothers.

Eric and Reece Wheeler had been operating in the district for over ten years, trading in anything from pigs' feet to gold dust and always at a profit. Their biggest moneyspinner was possum skins and not without good reason. When the market was low the Wheeler brothers would buy up skins like there was no tomorrow. They were never short of customers because they would always offer 5 percent over the going rate and it was nothing for them to buy anything up to 50,000 skins in one hit. The end result, though, was always the same.

Within three or four weeks of any one of their buying sprees fur prices would rise dramatically leaving the Wheelers counting their profits and laughing all the way to the bank while the trappers bemoaned their losses and cursed themselves for not hanging onto their skins for a little bit longer. Eric and Reece reckoned they were just lucky but we all knew there had to be something more to it than that.

Even though he had to travel a fair distance and it must have been a hassle in that clapped out Morrie of his, Garry kept up with his lessons. Most of what little work I had on at the time was in town so it was over a month before I dropped in on him again. The weather had been kind but all the same Garry must have been working like a Trojan because he already had over a thousand skins hanging in my old man's woolshed. Fur prices were still low and most of his skins were third grade smalls and mediums so I tried talking him into being a bit more selective. 'There's as much labour involved in getting a third grade skin ready as a first grade,' I told him, 'so until the market picks up, Garry, you'd be better off concentrating on first grade large and mediums and second grade large. You'll make almost as much money that way and have more time to go pighunting.'

Garry could see the merit in what I was saying but I knew he wasn't about to change his ways just yet. Like a lot of young blokes new to the game he was getting a bigger sense of achievement out of quantity rather than quality, and as for those two dogs of his they were getting plenty of exercise going by the number of lower jaws I could see hanging on the fenceline. They had both developed as hard bailers, with Missy taking on the extra duty of finder.

Garry was rapt in the way they'd turned out and thanked me all over again. I was quite rapt too, so I let him. By the end of August Garry had trebled his skin tally, doubled his jaw collection and had taken up fly tying in his spare time. I was surprised he had any. With spring just around the corner work started trickling in so I called round to see if Garry wanted his old job back. He was in the woolshed having a yarn about something with my old man and the Wheeler brothers were there too trying to sell a truckload of second-hand tyres that nobody wanted.

The old man was doing a good job of ignoring them and I did the same. The Wheelers finally took the hint and left. They hadn't been too interested in Garry's skins either so I figured there wasn't a price hike scheduled for the immediate future.

Despite this, and the fact that summer trapping is seldom profitable, Garry politely refused my offer of a job in favour of carrying on doing what he was doing. 'Skin prices have got to go up some time,' he predicted, which was true, but I wondered how much longer he could keep on going without some kind of an income. Getting my job offer turned down put my nose out of joint a bit but it taught me not to take people for granted.

Garry wanted to shift his line over to the next ridge so I gave him a hand and we found time to give his dogs a run. They were a good working pair all right. No sooner would you be sticking the first pig they'd found than they'd be off looking for another. My only criticism was the way Bruce went in on the snout, just a bit too direct and confident for my liking. I'd seen too many like him cut down in their prime and there's not much you can do with a dog like that except hope he gets a taste of the ivory early. Nothing so bad that he gets the guts knocked out of him but enough so he learns a bit of sense.

We got four pigs for five hours' hunting which was pretty good for the area but failed to score anything sizeable, the biggest being a boar of about 120 pounds. We had another hunt two weeks later where the dogs got onto a sow that attacked them. They weren't very impressed with that. It took them a while to get a hold then Garry called them off and let the sow go. They weren't very impressed with that either and skulked off somewhere to have a sulk. It worked too because that's all we got for the day, which hacked Garry off because he was nearly out of fresh meat. To save him from having a sulk I took him into town and shouted him a feed of fish and chips, then dropped him off later on that night.

With so much work coming in and most of it from the other side of the valley it was months before I saw Garry again. When I called round he and the old man were yarning in the woolshed like they were the last time, the only difference being the Wheelers weren't there. They had been there though, this time trying to sell rolls of fencing wire. They still hadn't shown any interest in Garry's skins which wasn't very good news for the young bloke, all things considered. He had over 5,000 of them but with the market at rock bottom they were about as much use as the blowflies they were attracting. He'd run out of money two or three months before so he'd done a bit of shearing for the old man just so that he could keep going. I couldn't help thinking that trapping had become a labour of love for young Garry — he wasn't making any money at it — though he seemed happy enough with the situation and still confident that a substantial price rise was just around the corner.

I was half-pie thinking of inviting him out on a hunt but he mumbled something about having to fix his car and went off to fix whatever it was that needed fixing. 'He's a tiger for work,' was my old man's comment, and nobody could argue with that.

A few minutes later Ted Thompson dropped in and the three of us hung around for two hours talking football and complaining about never having enough time to do anything. Just as I was leaving I noticed a manila folder lying on the work bench. 'The Wheelers left it behind,' my old man explained. 'Young Garry spotted it after they left. I thought they'd have come straight back for it but they didn't so it can't be worth anything.'

Like everybody else in the valley I didn't owe the Wheelers any favours but as I was going into town anyway I grabbed the folder with the intention of dropping it off on my way. By the time I'd got to town I'd forgotten all about dropping it off and only remembered it when I got home. I tossed it on the kitchen table as I walked in and put the kettle on for a brew. To make room for a plan I needed to look at regarding a job that had to be started that week, I shoved everything on the table to one side, and even though I tried to be careful some of the stuff ended up on the floor, the manila folder among them. It was full of receipts, sales dockets, that kind of stuff and they went spewing out all over the place.

Cursing the ktichen table for not being big enough I bundled them together and shoved them back into the folder. That's when I noticed the telegrams. Now I would like it to go on record that I'm not in the habit of reading other people's mail but those telegrams would have aroused anybody's curiosity. For a start some of them were quite old, going back five or six years, and they seemed to be in some kind of a code. The first one I picked up read: 20, 14, 5, 3, 18, 5, 16, 25, 20, 6, 9, 6, 16, 21, Sunlight soap. This didn't make much sense but neither did the next one, which read: 20, 14, 5, 3, 18, 5, 16, 25, 20, 18, 9, 8, 20, 16, 21, Wattie's peaches.

There were six telegrams altogether, all of them much along the same lines and all signed off with some well-known brand name like Bell tea or Edmonds baking powder, that kind of thing. I wasn't just curious any more; more like totally engrossed. Deciphering codes can be a satisfying and rewarding mental exercise or a sheer waste of time, depending on how good you are. At six o'clock that evening I spread all six telegrams out on the table and scrutinised them very carefully, looking for a common denominator because that's what Sherlock Holmes would have done and he was my boyhood hero who always got things right.

By midnight I had discovered that all six had three things in common besides being a lot of numbers and signed off with a consumer product. Number one was that they had been sent to the Wheelers care of their business address in town which didn't really mean much because that's where they lived. Number two, they had all been sent from different parts of the country, and number three, I still didn't have a clue what they were supposed to mean. After copying them down carefully I shoved the originals back into the folder and dropped them off into the Wheelers' place next morning.

Neither of the brothers was there, just an old bloke called Alfie Kidd who cleaned up and did odd jobs around the place. 'Just dropping this off, Alfie,' I said, handing over the folder. Alfie came to attention, threw his shoulders back and shoved the folder under his arm. For a second I thought he was going to salute me. 'You can rest assured that these documents will be passed on to my employers,' he said in officious tones, obviously enjoying the moment. Not that I blamed him for that though. The closest Alfie had ever got to handling the paperwork was putting a new toilet roll in the dunny. 'I know I can rely on you, Alfie,' I said, walking out the door, and that really made his day.

I spent every evening that week trying to decode those telegrams, or at least the copies I'd made of them. I'd been very careful in writing everything down. In addition to the messages in their entirety I'd also noted the dates and times of when they were sent and where they were sent from. At first none of this meant anything though I did notice that the Sunlight soap telegram had been sent from Stratford, the one signed Edmonds baking powder had come from Edgecumbe and the Wellington one had been signed Wattie's peaches. Maybe I was clutching at straws here but it seemed peculiar that the first letter of the product name matched the first letter of the town or city from where they were sent. Like the Bell tea one that had come from Blenheim and the last two signed Tip Top ice cream and Colman's mustard which had been sent from Tauranga and Cambridge respectively.

If I was right in my suspicions then the matching up of the first letters of both the place and product name could have been a code in itself. Something cooked up between the Wheelers and whoever it was sending the telegrams. That way the Wheelers would know that the messages were genuine.

Maybe this was a bit over the top as well but then I asked myself why were the telegrams sent in code in the first place if the Wheelers weren't trying to hide something? I mucked around with the numbers for another couple of days using every kind of mathematical combination I could think of but it didn't do any good. I was about ready to chuck it in and save myself a nervous breakdown when young Scott Pullen called in to say hello.

Scott was well known for his cheerful and optimistic nature but right then he looked anything but happy so I let him talk it out. A career as a pilot in the Royal New Zealand Air Force had been Scott's lifelong ambition and although he'd studied hard and had all the academic levels required he had failed his medical because of his eyesight. It just wasn't up to scratch. Poor Scott was heartbroken. 'That's the way it is with the air force, Charger,' he said. 'If you're A1 you're in, if you're B2 you might get in, but if you're classified as C3 or D4 you haven't got a hope.'

I should have been sympathising with young Scott right then, but I was over the moon. Without realising it Scott had helped me make a major breakthrough in deciphering the code. It was so simple I'd overlooked it completely. Number 1 was A, Number 2 was B, Number 3, C, and so on. I grabbed at one of the messages and invited Scott to take a look. I figured that by allowing Scott to help me with my problem he wouldn't have too much time to dwell on his own. Not that I expected to be thanked for it; after all that's what we're all here for, to help one another.

The telegram I picked at random was the one from Blenheim signed Bell tea and the numbers were as follows: 20, 14, 5, 3, 18, 5, 16, 25, 20, 6, 9, 6, 16, 21. Using the method of placing each letter as designated by the numbers in order I wrote out the word TNECREPYTFIFPU and took another step towards that nervous breakdown I was telling you about.

Thinking you've got a problem solved and then finding out you haven't knocks the wind out of a man faster than a blind hit. I tried rearranging the letters and using them with different number combinations I'd worked out before, but nothing fell into place. Scott had a go at it but he didn't do any good either and left shortly after to go and cry on somebody else's shoulder. I sat working away at the problem for another hour, then Betty Thompson called in. Two visitors in one day was a record for me, and for Betty Thompson to call in unannounced was very much out of the ordinary for her.

Being very reserved, prim and proper, Betty wasn't the type of woman who would normally visit a single man's home unchaperoned. After all, she was only 46, still waiting for Mr Right and didn't want to get herself a bad name. This time though she had a good reason for acting out of character. Her brother Ted had his fiftieth birthday coming up in a month and she wondered if I would help in 'arranging the festivities'. Did I think it a good idea to have everybody wearing a funny paper hat to add to the 'jollities', and if the weather was too hot she thought it wise to have plenty of raspberry cordial on hand so the men wouldn't have to drink so much beer to keep cool. All this had to be kept in the strictest confidence because she wanted it to be a surprise for Ted. It was going to be that all right.

As tactfully as I could I told Betty that it might be better if I arranged the liquid refreshments while she concentrated on the supper arrangements. She seemed happy enough with that and was about to leave when I showed her my TNECREPYTFIFPU word. 'What d'you make of this, Betty?' I asked.

Betty glanced at it momentarily. 'Oh, I see,' she said, 'this is perhaps a game for brother Ted's birthday party.'

'No, Betty, it's something I've been trying to work out,' I told her.

Betty took another look at the word. 'How silly,' she insisted, 'there's nothing to work out. Anyone can see it reads "Up fifty percent" spelt backwards.'

'Pardon?'

'This word of yours,' she repeated, tapping the paper. 'If you reverse the order of the letters it reads "Up fifty percent".'

I snatched up the paper and wrote out the letters in reverse order. Betty was right. It did read 'Up fifty percent'. Surely this time the code had been cracked. I went through all the other messages and they were all similar, though the actual rate differed. The Tip Top ice cream message said 'Up thirty percent' while the Colman's mustard one gave the highest rate of 'Up sixty-five percent'. 'You're a diamond, Betty,' I said, 'but what do you think it refers to?'

Betty didn't even have to think about that. 'Obviously it refers to something like share prices on the stock market, or perhaps wool prices —'

'— Or possum skins,' I interrupted. It had to be that, I was sure of it.

The Wheelers had always made a killing on possum skins by knowing exactly when to buy — now I knew how they knew. They were getting inside information from somebody who was in a position to give them that information well before anyone else had it, and this somebody was no doubt getting a cut of the profits for his troubles.

Out of sheer gratitude I gave Betty a big hug and a kiss on the cheek, which made her blush. We then had a cup of tea to celebrate because she never drank anything stronger. Then I walked her home because she didn't think a 'girl' should be seen walking alone after dark in case some people got the idea she had loose morals. 'Quite right, too,' I told her.

The next morning I raced out to see Garry. I couldn't wait to tell him and everybody else in the district all about the scam the Wheelers had been using. As per usual the old man was in the woolshed but this time he was on his own and actually working, shovelling some sheep dags into a wool pack.

'G'day, Dad, where's Garry?'

The old man put his glasses on just to make sure I was me before answering. 'He's left the district, son — gone to live in Opotiki, over there in the Bay of Plenty, on the East Coast.'

'I know where it is, Dad, but it's a bit sudden, isn't it,' I said, 'him leaving like that?'

The old man shook his head. 'Don't know about that; I think he had it planned. Last time you were here when he was working on his car he told me he was taking a trip over that way. He left that night then came back three days later, sold all his skins to the Wheelers, put all your boards and traps back in the shed here and then left. He said to thank you for everything and to look him up if you were ever over in the Bay of Plenty.'

'Did he get a good price for his skins?' I asked, not sure that I really wanted to know the answer.

'Too right, he did,' the old man grinned, putting down his shovel and reaching for his tobacco tin. 'The Wheelers came in here and straight away offered young Garry twenty-five percent over the current rate for all his skins — and he had over five thousand of them. I thought the young joker would take it but he told the Wheelers to shove their twenty-five percent and wouldn't take anything less than a hundred percent over current prices. The Wheelers argued a bit but in the end they paid up and handed over more than two and a half thousand quid [five thousand dollars plus] in cash. As soon as they left Garry got on the phone and rang every other trapper in the district and told them to hold out for a hundred percent too, and according to what I've been hearing all week, that's what they did.'

'The Wheelers paid in cash?' I asked, just a little bit incredulous.

'Yeah, they had a big box of the stuff, all fivers and tenners. Maybe they were trying to work some kind of a tax dodge, I don't know, but they had it with them, I know that. Then they went round buying up all the other skins in the district. It must have been costing them a fortune too — they were running out of cash at one stage and they had to get a loan off the bank using their place in town as collateral.'

'I wouldn't shed any tears over the Wheelers, Dad,' I said, 'considering what we know about them. It's a safe bet that skin prices are going to reach an all-time high.'

'Could be, son,' the old man agreed, 'but I was in town yesterday and bumped into old Alfie Kidd. He reckons the Wheelers are racing around in a mad panic looking very worried and spending a fortune on toll calls to the people who run the fur auctions down in Dunedin.'

'What do you mean, in a panic?'

'Just what I said. Near as I could make out the Wheelers have come a gutser this time. They've paid out a fortune on about fifty thousand skins that aren't worth a damn. I told Alfie to tell the Wheelers that if they were passing this way again to drop in and pick up the folder they left behind. I meant to drop it off myself but I forgot to take it in.'

'Hang on a minute, Dad,' I interrupted. 'You say the Wheelers left another folder behind. Have you still got it?'

'Yeah, it's right here on the bench. Right where they left it after they paid Garry for his skins.'

I picked up the folder and while my old man occupied himself with the wool pack he'd just filled with sheep dags I had a sneaky look inside. The latest telegram was on the top, dated nine days before, and it didn't take me long to decode the message. I'd had plenty of practice. 'Up two hundred percent' it read, and that didn't surprise me in the least, because the telegram had been sent from Opotiki and was signed 'Oxo beef stock cubes'.

CHAPTER 9

Calling Card

When Roy Lemmon called in at my old man's place looking for work he got taken on at face value, because that's the kind of bloke my old man was. He didn't even bother asking Roy for his name; Roy had to volunteer it. As my old man said many a time, a man can change his name to whatever suits, so there's no point in asking it in the first place.

At first we thought Roy was just another drifter who would take off after a month or so or when things got busy, round lambing or docking time, but Roy stuck around. He was tall and gangly, aged about thirty, and had ears that stuck out like a pink taxi with both the back doors open. But he had a lot of talent too. After just six months the old man was wondering how he'd ever got by without him.

No matter what job the old man gave him Roy could handle it like he'd been doing it all his life. He was a better than average drainlayer, a handy carpenter, good with stock, an expert horseman, first class shearer, an A grade mechanic and the best practical joker we'd ever had in the valley bar none.

Some of Roy's jokes were a bit borderline but they were never nasty or dangerous and he had the knack of being able to put one over on you even when you were expecting it and keeping a wary eye on him. He also had the knack of never being around when you got caught out on one of his jokes, which is the hallmark of the accomplished practical joker, but you always knew it was him because he'd leave his calling card. If you got into your vehicle to find that somebody had coated the steering wheel with axle grease then there'd be a lemon sitting on the seat. Or if you had trouble putting your trousers on in the morning because someone had sewn the bottoms together you'd find a lemon in one of the pockets.

One of Roy's borderline stunts happened on New Year's Eve, 1955. We were having our New Year's Eve dance down at the Community Hall, the same as we did every year, when unbeknown to the rest of us somebody put a hidden microphone in the ladies' toilet and connected it to one of the speakers in the hall. About half an hour before midnight, when most of us were well tanked up, the band were taking a break and more than half the women were in the Ladies, the same somebody flicked a switch. Talk about embarrassing. Some of the things we heard that night coming from the mouths of our genteel and respectable womenfolk were enough to make a grown man blush. Most of us did. It put the damper on things a bit and by the time the clock struck midnight there were only about a dozen of us left to sing Auld Lang Syne. We all knew Roy was responsible because he was nowhere around and after everybody had gone home Sammy Mita found a lemon sitting on top of one of the cisterns in the ladies' toilet. It was a while before the shockwaves from that little incident died down but Roy still had a trick or two up his sleeve.

After I moved into town, Roy moved into the old gardener's cottage I'd been using and my old man made no secret of the fact that he wanted Roy to stay on to take over as manager one day. For his part, Roy didn't seem too averse to the idea and started doing all the things a bloke would do if he intended sticking around. He spruced up the cottage with a coat of paint, opened a savings account with the Post Office, bought himself a 1936 model Chevy Coupe from a dealer in town, and mounted a couple of dog boxes on the back. Then before I could stop him he handed over a month's wages to Jock Woods for a pair of so-called finder/holder/bailers that I knew weren't even worth feeding. Everybody in the valley knew better than to deal with Jock Woods and Roy soon found out why.

'They're worse than useless, Charger,' Roy told me when I called round to see him three weeks later. 'I've had them out a dozen times behind Tennents Creek where it's crawling with pigs and neither of these two pot-lickers have shown a skerrick of interest. I don't think they even know what a wild pig looks like.'

'You're probably right about that, mate,' I said. 'Jock Woods has been taking good money for useless dogs for as long as anyone round here can remember and you haven't got a chance in hell of getting a refund either. He'll argue that he sold those dogs to you in good faith and that you ruined them with bad handling. You could try taking it out of his hide but that'll end up costing you more because he'll slap an assault charge on you, nothing surer. About the best thing to do is just cut your losses, and put it all down to experience.'

'It might be the best thing to do, Charger,' Roy agreed with a slow grin, 'but it doesn't have to be the only thing now, does it.'

Going by that remark I could only guess that Roy had something special in mind for Woods and on the following Friday we all found out what it was. It was Woods's habit to go into town on the last Friday of every month to catch up on his shopping and put a bet on down at the pub. But this time he was obliged to change his plans. He was about halfway down his drive, and picking up speed in his lumbering great Plymouth, when he was brought to a sudden stop, which slammed him against the steering wheel and was followed by an almighty thundering crash from behind. Somebody had tied one end of a long rope to the towbar of his Plymouth and had strategically fastened the other end to the exact centre of the supporting truss of his implement shed. The result was catastrophic. The entire roof structure had collapsed taking the rear wall with it and Woods was not amused.

The dust had hardly settled before everybody in the valley had got to hear about it. My mate Sammy Mita and I went up to take a look at the damage, more out of curiosity than anything else. Woods had been on the phone to everybody demanding to know who was responsible and claiming that his new shed was a complete write-off. He was half right about that. His shed was at least thirty years old and hadn't been that well built in the first place, but it was a write-off all right. By the time Sammy and I arrived there was already quite a crowd picking their way through the mess of twisted iron, shattered glass and broken timbers so we decided to keep well out of the way.

'This is a bit over the top even for Roy,' Sammy whispered, after first making sure no one was within earshot.

'We might be jumping to conclusions, mate,' I said. 'How do we know for certain that it was Roy?'

'It was Roy all right,' Sammy assured me. 'Take a look for yourself.'

I followed Sammy's gaze, and there in plain view on top of Woods's chopping block sat a single lemon. How everybody else missed seeing it, God only knows. Most probably too occupied going through the wreckage or something. I sauntered over and put the lemon in my pocket without anyone noticing, then Sammy and I headed off for town. Whereas I couldn't condemn Roy for what he'd done, I wasn't so sure I condoned his actions either. True, he had been ripped off, but like Sammy had said, Roy's vengeance had been a bit over the top. You wouldn't want to get on the wrong side of a joker like that.

Things quietened down after a few days like they always do, though I was still mystified as to how Roy had pulled it off. Getting within fifty yards of Woods's place without setting his dogs off would have been impossible for most people, yet Roy had been there, most probably at night, when dogs are more likely to kick up a racket, and he'd been working within just a few feet of them. A clever piece of work that.

Roy was pretty busy over the next few weeks or so with lambing and docking but as soon as things eased up a bit I took him into town to meet a breeder I knew. Almost at once he settled for a pair of lab crosses called Mike and Duke. The breeder was honest enough to admit that they were only young dogs with limited experience but Roy's mind was made up. As soon as we got back we gave them a run with my pack and for a pair of young dogs with limited experience they didn't do too badly. Duke was something special. He stayed keen and active the whole time, always looking for work, and didn't hold back on either of the two boars we got that afternoon. Roy was no slouch either. You could tell he'd done his share of pighunting just by the way he handled himself though he was reluctant to talk about it. The most I could get was, 'Did a bit on the East Coast a few years back.'

Maybe if I'd pushed it I could have learnt more, but I didn't want to seem like I was prying even though I was. You have to admit though, most pighunters like to talk about past hunts, the places they've been to and the different dogs they've owned over the years, but Roy wasn't like that. Pretty unusual really, especially for a bloke so keen on the sport and Roy was keen all right. That afternoon hunt with me had reawakened his hunting spirit, which I suspected had been dormant for far too long, and he went straight into overdrive like he was desperate to make up for lost time. He bought himself another dog off a bloke from Ohakune and was out running the three of them at every opportunity.

Though he didn't neglect his work. The old man was still happy with the way Roy was handling things on the place, even though he joked about him spending more time hunting than working, so he more or less handed over the reins and put him on a manager's salary.

Roy must have felt as though he had arrived. Everything was going well for him. He even had a girlfriend. Her name was Fiona Ridley and she worked in the town post office. A nice girl and even though she was a bit on the plain side Roy didn't have cause to complain, as he hadn't been first in line when looks were being handed out either. On Tuesday nights he drove into town and, along with Fiona and her parents, played cards at the bridge club. On Friday nights they left Fiona's parents at home and went to the movies. This, and the occasional Sunday drive, made up their social life, which wasn't much but they seemed happy enough. In fact just three months later they announced their engagement looking a picture of premarital bliss, and things were really moving in the valley.

With wool and meat prices holding high and steady there was that much work on, a man could get a job anywhere. The itinerant farm labourers who had been turned away during the years of the great Depression were now being welcomed with open arms. They came on foot or in an assortment of vehicles from towns and cities, the experienced and inexperienced alike. Most of them were okay, prepared to give a fair day's work for a fair day's pay, but we saw our share of no-hopers as well. The trouble was you could never tell how a bloke was going to turn out just by looking at him, but that wasn't worrying my old man anymore; he was leaving all the hiring and firing to Roy.

I called in to say hello one day after hanging a new pair of doors on Ted Thompson's old car shed and turned up about the same time as a bloke wearing two days' growth on his chin and a dirty shirt two sizes too big. He said he was looking for work, sounding quite desperate, and gave his name as John Bright but he didn't look it. The old man shouted him a cup of tea and admitted there was plenty of work going but told John the final decision was up to Roy.

'You can go and have a word with him after you finish your tea,' my old man offered. 'He's down at the cottage fixing something.'

I wanted to call in at the cottage myself to pick up a bit of gear I'd left behind so I waited while John helped himself to three cups of tea and twice as many smokes from my packet of Park Drive. Besides being broke and in need of a shave and a bath John Bright wasn't too fit either. It was only a ten minute slightly uphill walk to the cottage but it just about did for him. When we got there Roy was up a stepladder putting the finishing touches to a neat soldering job he'd done on the spouting.

'G'day Roy,' I greeted him. 'Brought somebody over for you to have a chat with. John Bright, meet Roy Lemmon.'

Roy turned around and just for a second I could have sworn there was a flash of recognition in his eyes but he and John shook hands like they were meeting for the first time so I figured I was imagining things. Most probably a case of John looking like someone Roy used to know. It happens. After picking up my gear there was nothing else for me to do except leave and let Roy and John talk things over. Besides, I got the feeling I was in the way, or maybe I was getting paranoid in my old age.

Over the next two months I was flat out in town. I didn't get out to see my folks until Christmas, and my old man wasn't too happy with Mr Bright.

'That bloke ought to be a taxidermist,' he said. 'All he does around here is stuff things. I don't know why Roy keeps him on — he's about as much use as an outbreak of facial eczema.'

'If he's so useless, Dad,' I said, 'maybe you should take it on yourself to send him down the road.'

My old man shook his head. 'I can't do that, son, it would be undermining Roy's authority, though to be honest he doesn't seem to have much of that as far as John Bright is concerned. In fact it's almost the other way round. He's been carrying that no-hoper since day one and on top of that he lends him the money to buy a truck, a Bedford three tonner. He reckons John is getting set to start his own firewood business but I've got my doubts about that and I still don't see why Roy had to lend him the money. He's got no hope of getting it back from that mongrel, mark my words.'

I stayed with my folks for a week, which was long enough to see that my old man hadn't been overstating matters. If John Bright had done any work around the place, then he'd done a good job of disguising the fact. When Sammy Mita called in for a Christmas and New Year beer I managed to get him outside for a quiet word.

'It's a weird situation, Charger,' Sammy said, lifting the top off a bottle of DB with his belt buckle. 'It's as if John is running the show. He just does whatever he feels like doing, which is never much, and takes off into town whenever he feels like it. Only last week they had a big mob of ewes to put through the dip and John took off for the races even before the job was half done. It's weird all right.

'There's other things too,' Sammy went on. 'Before John turned up Roy was out with his dogs every second day and feeding half the valley with wild pork but not anymore; he reckons he's too busy and he most probably is, what with him having to do all his own work and most of Bright's too. In fact he's so flat out these days he doesn't even have time to plant the lemon. It's been weeks since he pulled one of his stunts on anybody.'

'It's weird all right, Sammy,' I agreed, 'and there has to be a reason. Can you think of any?'

Sammy took a long pull on his bottle then began to roll a smoke one-handed. I've only ever met two men who could do that and one of them was a woman.

'I'll tell you what I think, Charger,' Sammy said, putting a match to his cigarette. 'I think Roy and John have known each other from way back and, what's more, I think John has got something on Roy, some kind of a hold and he's putting the pressure on. You could say he's squeezing the lemon.'

'I'll go along with that too, Sammy,' I said. 'But there isn't a lot anybody can do unless Roy asks for our help and I don't think he's going to do that.'

There wasn't much more Sammy and I could discuss about the problem, so we didn't try, we went pighunting instead. It was one of those spur of the moment things and I wasn't too hopeful as my dogs were back in town and Sammy was breaking in a new finder. But we did okay, more than okay in fact. Sammy's new finder, a kelpie cross called Tassie, which I didn't like the look of and Sammy had to keep whacking with a big stick to stop him picking fights with the other dogs, turned out to be surprisingly good at his job. Quite a specialist in fact. He didn't just go for any pig — he concentrated on boars only. Sammy reckoned Tassie had done the same thing the previous times he had taken him out. He was really over the moon just because his new dog could tell the difference between a boar and a sow. I couldn't see what all the fuss was about; I'd been able to do that for years.

We got three boars that day, two of them around the 130-pound mark and looking like your typical Captain Cooker, but the third one was a bit out of the ordinary. Big and ginger with only one eye, one ear and one broken tusk. He walked straight through the dogs like they weren't even there and had a go at Sammy and me like he meant business. He most probably did. I could have ended things without any trouble if I'd had my Marlin but all we had between us was Sammy's beat-up single-shot .22 which only went off when it felt like it. For what seemed like forever the boar took turns at charging the dogs and us while Sammy took pot-shots at it with his .22 which had no effect whatever. Finally one of the dogs managed to get a hold and Sammy jumped in like greased lightning and stuck it behind the shoulder. Neither of us, or any of the dogs, had any injuries to speak of but we were all shaken up by the experience.

Getting that boar back to the truck just about crippled Sammy and me but we were glad we made the effort. It weighed 241 pounds gutted, which though not considered exceptional for those times still added up to a lot of pork. It was the first sizeable boar for the New Year so we had it entered into the club records. We honestly thought one of the boys would get a bigger one before long, but strangely enough none of them did until four years later. The big boars were getting harder to come by.

Sammy said he could get a lift from one of the blokes at the clubhouse back to my parents' place to pick up his truck so I told him I'd see him later and headed off for town. I was looking forward to a hot bath, a change of clothes and a night out at the movies.

Making good time in the old Ford, I was only ten minutes away from the main highway when I noticed the Bedford parked on the wrong side of the road, with the bonnet up and John Bright leaning against the driver's side door rolling a smoke. I didn't really want to stop but I did, and saw a pair of legs sticking out from under the chassis. They belonged to Roy Lemmon.

In view of everything my old man and Sammy had been saying I suppose it was only natural to have Roy under the truck fixing the problem while John stood around doing nothing to help. But that didn't stop me getting hot under the collar about it. I gave Bright a look that said I'd punch his lights out if he so much as opened his mouth and crawled under the truck to see if I could lend a hand.

'It's not much of a problem really, Charger,' Roy explained. 'Just a hole in the fuel line. I'll just bind it up with insulation tape. It'll do for now but John will have to get it repaired properly before too long or the petrol will just eat through the tape.'

It wasn't really a two man job but I stayed under the truck with Roy until he'd finished and then continued on into town while he and John presumably headed back to the farm.

The week-long stay with my folks and the hunt with Sammy had been a tonic and I made up my mind that night to get out to the valley at least once a month no matter how much I had on in town. By working a 60-hour week and taking on an extra tradesman I was able to stick with the plan, though only just, and quite a bit happened in that next 30-day period.

My folks had been away visiting relatives in Wellington and didn't know the full story, but between them and Sammy I was able to get a fairly clear picture of what had taken place. It seemed that with my folks away John had decided to do even less work on the place and by this time Roy had had a gutsful. He told John to either shape up or ship out. There was a blazing argument which resulted in Roy kicking John off the place, but it didn't end there.

As soon as John got into town, he went straight round to see Fiona and her parents. He told them that Roy had done a twelve-month stretch in Mt Eden for theft as a servant while working as a night porter for a high-class Auckland hotel. Roy Lemmon was definitely not a man to be trusted, he said. At first neither Fiona nor her parents would believe it but Fiona's old man, who had more connections than a Telecom switchboard operator, made some inquiries and it all turned out to be true. There was a hell of scene over that lot, with Fiona and her mum crying and her dad threatening all kinds of legal action. Roy tried to explain that it had all been a stupid mistake he'd made a long time ago, that he'd paid his debt to society and had never been in any kind of trouble since, but it didn't do any good. Fiona called off the engagement and her old man threatened to gut-shoot Roy if he so much as came within a mile of his daughter. She wasn't going to marry some no-good ex-jailbird and that was all there was to it. Poor Roy was heartbroken. He drove back to the cottage that night, collected his things, dropped his dogs off at Sammy's place and left the valley without even saying goodbye to anybody.

'Nobody knows where he's got to,' Sammy told me. 'But according to rumour, John Bright has scored himself a job with a bush gang somewhere near Taupo.'

I couldn't have cared less where John Bright was except that maybe he'd know where to find Roy and if I could get that information from him then maybe I could talk Roy into coming back to work on the farm. He'd been happy there and we were all missing the pranks he'd caught every one of us out on at one time or another.

'Always leaving a lemon behind just to let us know it was him was a classic move.' Sammy grinned nostalgically. 'I think he'll be remembered more for that than anything else.'

'You're not wrong there, Sammy,' I said.

Finding myself in Taupo one month later had nothing to do with John Bright or Roy Lemmon. I was chasing up a rumour about a 500-pound boar that had allegedly been shot by a couple of deer-stalkers up near the headwaters of the Waitahanui. I found out at the pub that it was all a scam. The general gist of it was, a couple of jokers had stolen the boar from a pig farm in Huntly and had tried entering it into a Taupo pighunting competition for the prize money. Obviously they knew nothing about wild pigs. Quite apart from the fact that any pighunter could see that the boar had been a tame one, bred on skim milk and pellets, the two would-be prize winners hadn't even taken the ring out of its nose. The publican at the Taupo pub said that if I wanted to see a real wild boar, that had weighed in at 314 pounds, I should take a drive out to the Highway Hotel.

'It's just a few minutes out of town on the way to Napier,' he said. 'They've got it hanging up in the chiller.'

With nothing better to do I drove out there and arrived just in time to be too late.

'We had it here for a few days,' explained the barman, who introduced himself as Gavin. 'But the jokers who got it came and picked it up about half an hour ago.'

'That's the way it goes,' I said, mostly because I couldn't think of anything more intelligent to say.

As I was already there it was only natural to have a beer and as I was his only customer Gavin insisted I have it on the house.

'It's hard to believe,' he said, filling up two eight-ounce glasses, 'but by four o'clock this place will be bursting at the seams with bushmen. There must be at least a dozen gangs working within a five mile radius of this place and they're a thirsty bunch.'

'Tell me, Gavin, have you come across a bloke by the name of John Bright?' I asked. 'I hear he's working with a gang in these parts.'

'He was working around here,' Gavin corrected me. 'But not any more. He topped himself just over a week ago. Saturday before last, in fact. He'd been in here most of the day, drinking with a tall skinny bloke with jug ears, till about three o'clock. That's when they parted company. The skinny bloke heads for town in his Chevy Coupe and John decides to drive back to his camp on the other side of Punai Gorge just behind us here.'

At this point Gavin stuck his thumb over his shoulder to indicate where Punai Gorge was.

'It's hard to say exactly what happened after that,' he continued.

'The only witnesses were a couple of fishermen walking back from the river and they'd spent most of the afternoon sucking on a bottle of Scotch. According to them John had just started going downhill in that three tonner of his when the motor cut out. It's a long way to the bottom of Punai Gorge and with his motor not going John was in big trouble. He couldn't get the truck into gear, what with it having a crash box, and with no motor his brakes weren't operating either. The two fishermen reckoned he was fair flying by the time he got to the bottom of the gorge and didn't have a chance in hell of making the bend. He slammed head on into a bloody great rimu and was killed outright. Nobody could have survived that mess,' Gavin concluded, refilling our glasses. 'You only have to take a look at what's left of the truck to see that.'

'You mean it hasn't been towed away yet?' I asked.

'Not yet it hasn't,' Gavin answered. 'They dragged it out of the gorge soon enough — it was blocking off half the road — but then they parked it out the back here to try and find out what had caused the motor to cut out. It's been here since and I don't think anyone is interested in towing it away, not even for parts. The only ones happy about that are the chooks; they've adopted it as their new hen house.'

'Getting back to the motor problem, Gavin,' I said, 'did they find out what caused it?'

'Too right they did,' Gavin stated. 'But I doubt if any untrained person would have spotted it. The cause of the problem was a tiny hole in the fuel line, not much bigger than a match head.'

I don't know why but I started feeling just a little bit uncomfortable as Gavin refilled our glasses for the third time.

'If it's all right with you, Gavin, I'd like to have a look at what's left of the truck.'

'Help yourself, mate,' Gavin invited. 'Everybody else around here has but there's not much to see unless you like wrecks.'

I wandered out back, trying to appear more casual than I felt, and after making sure nobody was looking crawled under the wreckage to look at the fuel line. Finding the hole wasn't a problem — I knew where to look — but the thing I noticed first was the absence of adhesive tape.

When Roy had carried out the temporary repair in the valley that day he'd taken at least two dozen turns of the stuff around the fuel line yet there wasn't a trace of it left. It couldn't have just fallen off as cleanly as that; somebody would have had to remove it. I tried not to think what I was thinking but Gavin's description of the tall skinny bloke who had been drinking with John and who'd driven away in a Chevy Coupe kept nagging away at me. Thinking about something you don't want to think about gets harder when you have to do the thing that you don't want to do; but I had to do it. I couldn't get the doors of the cab open as they'd been jammed against the bodywork by the impact, so I climbed over the mangled mess of the bonnet and stuck my head through the windscreen. If there'd been a lemon sitting on the dashboard I would have freaked out for sure but thankfully there wasn't.

The floor of the cab was covered in shattered glass, just like you'd expect, along with a couple of old newspapers and a 'Best Bets' book, but nothing unusual or out of place except for the egg. It was sitting right in the middle of the driver's seat, but under the circumstances you couldn't say it was out of place. There were at least 20 hens scratching around close by and even a couple perched on the tray. Just like Gavin had said, they had commandeered the wreckage of the Bedford as their own unique hen house. I breathed a sigh of relief and promised myself never to jump to conclusions again. There was a rational explanation for everything and it hadn't been all that difficult to work out. The tall skinny bloke could have been anybody and there were a lot of Chevy Coupes getting around the country in those days. As for the missing adhesive tape, no mystery there either. Obviously it had been removed by the blokes inspecting the wreck. The logical explanation was that John had forgotten about the temporary repair to his fuel line, the petrol had eaten its way through the tape causing fuel starvation, and this had happened at the worst possible time. All very unfortunate but an accident pure and simple, with nobody to blame, least of all Roy Lemmon.

I walked back into the bar and had one last beer with Gavin before leaving, but I just had to clear up one thing.

'This tall skinny bloke you mentioned, Gavin,' I said. 'You don't know his name by any chance?'

Gavin shook his head.

'Sorry mate, I don't, but you shouldn't have any trouble finding that out. I hear he's working as the manager at Beech Holdings. It's a big property about three miles down the road from here and his place is the first one on the left after the turn-off to the river.'

I thanked Gavin for the information and free beer and left with every intention of heading for home but I didn't. Curiosity, I suppose. According to the speedometer on my Ford the Beech Holdings manager's residence was exactly three and two-tenths miles from the pub. It was a newly built house situated about a hundred yards back from the road. There was a Chevy Coupe with dog boxes mounted on the back parked outside which looked very familiar, as did the tall skinny bloke who was walking from the house to the woodshed. I now knew for sure that the tall skinny bloke who had shared John Bright's last hours on earth had been Roy but I wasn't about to jump to any more hasty conclusions. Just because Roy had been at the pub with John didn't mean he had anything to do with his death. I was convinced of it and I might have stayed convinced if I hadn't read the name on the mail box. 'Beech Holdings', it read. 'Manager's Residence — Roy Fowler.'